# THE CAVERN

# The Cavern

*A play by*
JEAN ANOUILH

*Translated by Lucienne Hill*

*A Spotlight Dramabook*
HILL AND WANG • NEW YORK

Manufactured in the United States of America by
The Colonial Press Inc., Clinton, Mass.

# THE CAVERN

# CHARACTERS

The Author
The Count
The Countess
Baron Jules
Baroness Jules
The Seminarist
The Superintendent
Romain, *the butler*
Marie Jeanne, *the cook*
Leon, *the coachman*
Marcel, *the valet*
Hugueline, *the chambermaid*
Adele, *the kitchen maid*
Alexis, *the scullery boy*
Nurse
Elder Boy
Younger Boy

# ACT ONE

*The set is in two parts. The bottom half is the kitchen, murky,
cavernous, with a ventilator giving on to the street through
which can be seen the feet of passers-by. Up above, spacious,
airy rooms. In the center room, a huge portrait of an old lady
in ceremonial dress. Nothing looks real in either of these sets.
Down in the kitchen, an enormous stove, with its big black
pipe rising incongruously right through the floor and up
through the rooms above, masking the portrait of the Old Lady
in her brocade dress.*

*When the curtain goes up, all the characters are on stage,
motionless. They seem to be waiting for something. The police
SUPERINTENDENT is downstairs among the kitchen staff: bowler
hat, high stiff collar, black suit. Beside him, the AUTHOR, whose
rather untidy present-day clothes stand out against the period
costumes of his characters.*

*After a moment of general hesitation the AUTHOR, a little
embarrassed, comes down to the footlights and addresses the
audience.*

AUTHOR. The play we are going to perform tonight is one I've
never succeeded in writing. I've written a great many others,
plays which you have been indulgent enough to applaud,
for close on thirty years now. [*He waits a second or two for
the applause which does not come, then says.*] Thank you.
. . . [*He goes straight on, a little vexed.*] But this one, I've
never been able to write. Even so, we're going to try to perform it. Yes, I know. You've paid for your seats without
knowing that little point. But those of you who aren't satisfied can ask for your money back at the end of the per-

7

formance. Well, that is, in theory . . . Because judging from the stampede at the box office these last few days, I think—to be perfectly honest—that the management hasn't quite worked out the exact procedure of reimbursement. Now, we've been practicing for four weeks. You haven't. And it's the audience who makes the play. I've always thought that we ought to rehearse the public and the press as well. We might have fewer flops. Unfortunately . . . Anyway, tonight's play isn't made. It's in the making. And we have great hopes of you. I can hear somebody whispering that this has already been done by Pirandello. Well, this isn't quite the same thing as you will see, and, furthermore, it only goes to prove that Pirandello had his problems, too. Yes, well now, the last time I spoke to the manager about this idea of giving customers their money back— in view of the unusual nature of our enterprise—he slapped me heartily on the back—and he said, "My dear maestro"— he calls me maestro this year because last year I had a success—the years when I have a flop he calls me "dear old darling"—"My dear maestro," he said, "you're too modest. The case won't even arise!" Anyhow, at least I've warned you. This play—had it been a real play—this play was to be called *The Cavern*. The Cavern to me, represents . . . Well, you'll see. To begin with: the set. I don't like complicated settings much, they always cover up some weakness. "The theatre," said Lope de Vega, "is two boards, two trestles, and a passion." The two boards and the two trestles are easy, you can always find those. But the passion, the true passion which turns seven or eight hundred individuals into one single attentive being, that's not so easily come by. Raggedy little shreds of passion, as a rule, tiny trickles which the author, sitting all by himself with his fountain pen, fondly thought of as a deluge. What I really wanted was no scenery at all, just the characters. But, there we are. The action takes place in a mansion in Paris, in the fashionable Faubourg St. Germain at the turn of the century. Down below we have the kitchen—the kitchen—the Cavern in fact, where lives the servant world. There were a great many of those at the time, in the houses of the best people. That portrait of a lady up there—that's the Old Girl, as they called her. She is the one-time mistress of the household. The Count's first wife. She's been dead a long time when the play opens, and she plays no visible role in it. But under her sway, the Cavern folk, badly fed, badly paid, and badly treated as they were, lived through a spell of hideous calm and peace of mind, which they hanker for in some vague way, now that their masters have become more human— under the influence of the second Countess—that fairhaired young lady up there on your right. So now, in this so far un- written play, we have the upper characters—it's quite easy, those are the ones who are upstairs in the set—and we have the lower characters, who are down below. The lower char- acters are the servants—plus the little priest. He isn't a priest actually. He's a seminarist, who hasn't taken Holy Orders yet. Why a seminarist? A dozen times the management asked me that. Make him a telegraphist, a contortionist, anything you like, only not a seminarist. There are enough questionable episodes in this blessed play as it is! Well, I'm sorry, no. He's a seminarist. You'll have to put up with it, just as I did. Temporarily included in the downstairs charac- ters, we also have the Police Superintendent. [He gives him a friendly little wave.] Hullo.

SUPERINTENDENT. Hullo. [To audience.] Mesdames, Mes- sieurs——

AUTHOR. An old acquaintance, that one. One of those facile, showy characters who has nothing to do with the plot, and whom I always put into my plays to help me begin. The play opened with him, just like a real play, before that black day when I gave up trying to write it. He called at the Count's house—the Count is that distinguished gentleman with the graying hair on the top floor—the day after the murder of the cook—— [*He breaks off.*] I didn't tell you, but the cook has been stabbed—at least I think so, I'm not sure yet—in circumstances which have never been very clear—even to me. [The SUPERINTENDENT *has discreetly gone off stage.*] They're coming down to play their first scene. [*The* SUPERINTENDENT *has appeared in the central room where the* COUNT *is standing.*] After that, we'll see. Off you go, then.

*He nods to the* SUPERINTENDENT *and retires into a corner. The lights dim in the basement and become brighter on the first floor. All the characters go out save the* COUNT *and the* SUPERINTENDENT, *who start their scene upstairs and continue it down in the kitchen, where the lights come up again.*

*The* COUNT *makes a gesture of resigned assent. They go down.*

SUPERINTENDENT. Here, was it?

COUNT. Yes, here. She was lying just there.

*The* SUPERINTENDENT *inspects the room gravely, stoops to pick up a thread, then throws it away, disappointed. He pulls out his notebook and some papers.*

SUPERINTENDENT. Let us go over the facts.

COUNT. Very well.

SUPERINTENDENT. I quite realize that it must be very unpleasant having to answer these questions, sir. The Prefect, in entrusting me with the task of pursuing this investigation, was most anxious, he told me so himself, to avoid any bespattering—even indirectly—of a name which forms, in some sense, a part of our national heritage. Those are the Prefect's very words. His choice of me is a policy in itself. I am on the files as having always been a right-thinking man, your Grace.

COUNT [*gravely*]. I congratulate you on it, Superintendent.

SUPERINTENDENT. Let us get down to business, your Grace.
We want to unearth the whole truth, so as to be in a position to—shall I say?—publish only a portion of it.

COUNT [*lightly*]. I have every intention of helping you do it,
Superintendent. The truth is a woman I adore: first, because
she is naked; and secondly, if I'm to believe most of her
painters, because she is young and comely—and who knows?
—perhaps a virgin, too.

SUPERINTENDENT. The truth, for us, means a watertight case.
Mine must hold water, your Grace. That's all I ask.

COUNT. We shall do our best to see it does, Superintendent.

SUPERINTENDENT. I see we understand each other as—shall I
say?—men of good breeding.

COUNT. You're too kind.

SUPERINTENDENT. An old woman gets done—a professional
term, your Grace—and quite obviously, although he denies
it, by her aging lover; no skin off anyone's nose. But they
send you, rather thoughtlessly, two fledgling inspectors—
who ask rather too many questions and we're landed with a
tale of abortion and white slavery, and a mysterious little
priest who stammers his way through his evidence and
makes me wonder just what he's doing here in the first
place. All that down in black and white on the report. If
this had happened in the suburbs . . . we'd have ten lines
on the center page, and that would be that. But here, in the
kitchens of one of the best-known aristocratic families in
Paris, well, for some folk, whom I won't name, the scandal,
if scandal there were, would be—shall I say?—a godsend?

COUNT [*losing patience*]. Say away, Superintendent, but may
I beg you to say it quickly. I am riding with a lady this
morning and I should hate to keep her waiting in the park.

SUPERINTENDENT. I'm—shall I say?—an ordinary man. [*He
smiles archly.*] But I know that one doesn't keep a lady

waiting. And that certain names are entitled to remain un-smirched. I am here to champion the cause of—silence. That's why I talk so much, as a matter of fact. I am ill at ease, as you might say. Excuse this rather personal question, your Grace, but were you ever your cook's lover?

COUNT [*smiling*]. She was an old woman by this time.

SUPERINTENDENT [*consulting his notes*]. Forty-seven years of age.

COUNT. But she was once the most exquisite young chamber-maid that the Countess, my first wife, ever unearthed from her country estates. She got all her maids there, and as ugly as sin they were too. In point of fact I never did under-stand this blunder in a woman who never committed any.

SUPERINTENDENT. Am I to take your answer in the affirmative, your Grace?

COUNT. I told you that years ago she was a beauty.

SUPERINTENDENT [*delicately*]. I won't press the point. How many years did you remain her lover?

COUNT. I don't think this detail will be of use to you, Super-intendent.

SUPERINTENDENT. Is it true to say that a son—shall I say a natural son?—was born of this union?

COUNT. All sons are natural sons, sir. I must, however, add that I didn't know of the boy's existence until the day of the drama itself.

SUPERINTENDENT. Quite so, let us come to the drama. It ap-pears that on the twenty-seventh of last month, around six-thirty in the evening, your other servants, on entering the kitchen, [*Reading from his papers.*] "found their fellow domestic, Ermeline Joseph, aged forty-seven, here employed as cook, lying on the floor of the said kitchen, bathed in her own blood. Witnesses all affirm that, during the hour preceding the discovery of the injured woman by her fellow domestics, two persons were seen talking to the said Ermeline

Joseph. To wit: Monsieur le Comte Xavier Stanislas Pierre Jean Thibaut de——"

*The* COUNT *gives an impatient wave of the hand.*

SUPERINTENDENT. . . . well, you, "and the young seminarist Thomas Joseph, natural son of the said cook. However, it must be pointed out that by common knowledge the said Ermeline Joseph had a lover, the coachman, Leon Lacase . . ." Did you know that?

COUNT. I paid very little attention to such details, Superintendent.

SUPERINTENDENT [*goes on reading*]. ". . . a brutal drunken character with whom she had frequent quarrels, often resulting in blows being . . . [*He peers at his papers.*] exchanged. . . ." This man managed to produce an alibi—shall I say? —unfortunately, as he was the ideal suspect. "Ermeline Joseph, questioned by Constable Simard in the course of her transfer to hospital, refused to give the name of her attacker. She died without it being possible to interrogate her further." [*He thumbs through his notes.*] Then we have the interrogation of the seminarist Thomas Joseph, who admits to having a violent scene with his mother. What was this boy's exact position in your household, your Grace?

COUNT. The Abbé who taught my children Latin was called away for two months. On Ermeline's recommendation we engaged this boy to take his place.

SUPERINTENDENT. Did you not know he was her son?

COUNT. Absolutely not.

SUPERINTENDENT. Or yours?

COUNT. Even less so. I think I told you that I only learned of his existence on the day of the tragedy.

SUPERINTENDENT. When you left the woman Joseph, was she still in her normal state?

COUNT [*after a slight hesitation*]. No, she was already wounded. . . .

*The* Superintendent *stops in confusion. A pause. He looks*
*at the* Count *with astonishment.*

Superintendent. That's an extremely important point, your
Grace. Do you mean you didn't raise the alarm? You didn't
call the police, or send for a doctor?
Count [*stiffly, suddenly*]. No.

*A pause.*

Superintendent. But do you realize the gravity of this fact?
Which is fortunately not recorded in your original state-
ment. [*He checks this in his notes and sighs with relief.*]
Count [*inscrutably*]. I realize it perfectly well. It's precisely
one of those things which one can hardly explain to the
police. There are a great many, even in the life of an honest
man.

*An embarrassed pause.*

Superintendent. The truth, for us, is a case that holds water.
And we have a few cards up our sleeves, thank the Lord.
First of all, the drunken coachman was her lover. He has
an alibi. But barkeeper's alibis—well, we all know what
they're worth. Secondly, there's Marcel Punais, your valet,
whose activities are not very clear between five and seven
o'clock on that day. A definitely shady character, that one,
frequents race courses and is in flagrant contact with a
procurer for brothels in North Africa. The said Punais having moreover made open attempts to get your young kitchen
maid Adele Lepied into such an establishment in Algiers.
According to the latest information, the Lepied girl is now
an inmate of this said establishment.
Count [*shrugging*]. She's left the household, that's all I know.
Superintendent. The man has therefore achieved his ends,
which doesn't argue in his favor. [*He gathers up his papers
and brief case.*] You don't seem to have much luck with
your servants, your Grace?

Count [*smiling*]. As you see.

*They have started up the stairs again.*

Superintendent. It's more and more difficult to find suitable domestics these days. I'm a man of modest means and my wife has to make do with a mere maid of all work, but she has a principle: she picks them over 180 pounds and swarthy.

Count. That was my first wife's principle too, as I told you. Only hers were sandyhaired and dwarfish. The world is crawling with them.

*They have gone out. They reappear, still talking, in the upper part of the set.*

Superintendent. Now let's be brief, your Grace. It would be a sorry thing indeed if a well-run police force started—shall I say?—molesting a respectable man, when it has two items of gallowsmeat to hand, who've already earned their ten-year stretch in any case. We are going to resume the interrogation with—shall I say?—modern methods. And I am confident that we'll get a confession from one or other of them, if not both.

Count [*a little tersely*]. There *is* something else I have to tell you, Superintendent.

Superintendent [*ambiguously*]. Your Grace, as one man of good breeding to another, I would rather you didn't tell me too much. Even with a watertight case, you must to some extent be able to believe in it yourself.

Count. I did not, needless to say, "do" my cook, as you put it, even if she did happen to be my mistress nearly thirty years ago; I found her injured. She refused to let me call a doctor. I knew, moreover, that she did not want to reveal the name of her attacker—out of a conception of honor which may strike you as a little [*He smiles.*]—shall I say?—unusual, but which exists in certain people; as I need hardly tell you.

There are some people who don't care for the police.

SUPERINTENDENT [*with sudden shrewdness*]. Your Grace, the police can do without the love of honest folk, but honest folk can't do without the police.

*The* COUNT *gives a kind laugh and pats the* SUPERINTENDENT *on the back.*

COUNT. I must say, I like you very much, Superintendent. Do your job as you see fit. But give your Prefect my respects and tell him, please, that I absolve him from all precautions on my account. I might possibly find them—shall I say?—insulting. I fully intend to be suspected on the same footing as everybody else, or I may take offense.

SUPERINTENDENT. Very good, your Grace.

COUNT. Now, if you'll excuse me . . .

SUPERINTENDENT [*very much the man of the world*]. One doesn't keep a lady waiting, your Grace. I know that!

COUNT [*smiling*]. At last a serious remark! I shan't see you out, Superintendent. As agreed, you are at home here.

[*He bows and goes out.*

SUPERINTENDENT [*anxiously*]. This business is going to be—shall I say?—thorny, for all its distinguished looks. It's all a matter of seeing things clearly, but not too clearly.

HUGUELINE *enters the drawing room, carrying a tray. He calls out:*

Mademoiselle!

HUGUELINE [*turning*]. Oh! How you scared me, sir!

SUPERINTENDENT [*twirling his mustache and sidling over to her*]. What do you usually do between five and seven, my pretty child?

HUGUELINE [*with a great show of confusion*]. Why, sir, I . . . [*She asks slyly.*] Are you a guest of his Grace the Count, sir?

SUPERINTENDENT. In a manner of speaking, my pretty child.

HUGUELINE [*simpering, but steely-eyed*]. In that case . . . if I'm detailed to the service of your room, sir, you've only to ring for me.

*She goes out, waggling her bottom. The* SUPERINTENDENT *watches her go with prodigious interest.*

SUPERINTENDENT. That's an interrogation which ought to produce something—by God!—something—shall I say?—h'm. I rather think I shan't say it.

*He follows her out, jubilantly twirling his cane. He discreetly reappears downstairs with the others shortly after* HUGUELINE; *he does not seem to recognize her, nor she him*

*The* AUTHOR *steps down to the footlights. A spot focusses on him.*

AUTHOR. And there we are. Up to this point it was more or less all right. We had an exposition scene that told one a fair amount, the action seemed to get under way. . . . But this cook, one of my main characters, was already dead when the curtain went up. [*Far upstage, the* COOK *appears silent, as if she were miles away, stirring some mysterious potion in a wooden mortar.*] Well, what would you have done? Continue the play without ever seeing her? It was possible. Sensible even. But it broke my heart. To begin with, I really loved the woman. In my notes I used to call her "Mother Earth." You remember Rimbaud's poem, "The Hands of Jeanne Marie."

> *Jeanne Marie has brawny hands,*
> *Tawny hands that summer tanned—*

[*He sighs.*] Marie Jeanne she was, in my mind. [*He exclaims suddenly.*] That's an idea! We'll call her Marie Jeanne; it's better than Ermeline, don't you agree? [*He looks at her.*] Marie Jeanne! It was to try and bring her to life again, to coax her out of the vague world of possibility and give her two cents' worth of reality, that I wanted to write this play. So it was out of the question to kill her before the curtain went up. . . .

*The other characters have all come in silently during his speech. They surround him dumbly, dotted all over the set, as if anxious about what he has decided to do. There is a moment of anguish as he stands there, hemmed in by them all. Then he catches sight of the* SUPERINTENDENT.

Only there was that wretched Superintendent with that waggish manner of his, jeopardizing the whole thing, the ape. [*He turns to the* SUPERINTENDENT *who is standing beside him, listening anxiously.*]

SUPERINTENDENT [*vexed*]. I daresay. But you can't say I came seeking *you* out, can you?

AUTHOR [*genuinely apologetic*]. I know. I'm entirely to blame, as always. I wanted to write a very simple, very innocent play, but somehow I can never do it. In an earlier version the play opened with Marie Jeanne alone in her kitchen in the early morning, greeting her son. That was good, too. Not so showy, but less contrived than that opening with the Superintendent. [*He comes to a sudden decision.*] Come on then! We'll play the other opening, too. And then we'll see. Clear the stage, everybody! We're playing the other opening.

*The characters who had come back timidly on stage during his monologue begin to go out somewhat reluctantly. He shouts after them:*

You'll be coming back! [*To the audience.*] These actors! When it isn't their turn to speak they're convinced there's no more play! Now. Here we are, in the big cool dark kitchen, very early in the morning. . . . In that indefinable, dispiriting smell that kitchens have before the stove is lit. In the dim Cavern stands the old firebrand over her ovens, up before anyone is stirring. Look at her. Mother Nature, old Earth Mother. She knows countless brews and broths. The secrets of sauces marvelous and murderous. The secret of potions, too. Potions to make a man love you—and potions to throw out the fruits of love afterwards. She is no ordinary cook. Look at her, look carefully. She is the Queen of the Cavern. She has an old gilt crown she keeps hidden under a pile of rags at the bottom of a cupboard. She'll show it to you. She shows it to everybody when she has a drink inside her. She really was a queen at twenty. A carnival queen. The loveliest thighs in Nice! They told her so when they gave her the prize. That was all over long ago, of course, but it has left her with an ancient pride. She is the aristocracy of the Cavern. So now, in this second opening, the little seminarist arrives in Paris, having been sent for by his mother. . . . [*He shouts to the actor playing the* SEMINARIST, *who appears in the low doorway.*] on you come, lad —his big peasant's hands hanging loosely from his sleeves. . . . He is the bastard. He doesn't know it yet, but he can feel, dimly, that he belongs neither above stairs nor below. That will be his drama. That is why he took refuge in God and why he hides under those robes of his. He felt that he couldn't bear just being a peasant. He's someone who always feels cold, this boy. But God is chilly and silent, too.

MARIE JEANNE *senses the presence of the* SEMINARIST *at the top of the stairs. She turns away from her stove and says briefly:*

MARIE JEANNE. Come in. No one's going to eat you. They're not agin' the cloth in this house. [*He looks down at her dumbly from the top of the stairs. She goes on.*] In the Old Girl's day, you had to come back with your chit signed by the priest on Sunday mornings or out you went! She wanted her pots and pans scoured by good Catholics. [*She says again, gruffly.*] Come in, do!

*The* SEMINARIST *comes downstairs. He sets his little suitcase
down at his feet.*

SEMINARIST. Good morning, Mother.

MARIE JEANNE. Morning, priest. You took the six o'clock train,
did you? Were you able to sleep?

SEMINARIST. No. It was very crowded. I stood in the corridor
and I had to change at three o'clock at Viezon. I waited
nearly an hour there. I could have slept in the waiting room,
only I was afraid I'd miss the connection.

MARIE JEANNE [*with a cheerful snort*]. You're always afraid
of something. Sit down. I'll give you some coffee. Some of
mine. The kind they'll never get upstairs. [*Grumpy, she
pours him a cup after deftly wiping a corner of the table.*]
There, you see, there's *some* justice down here on earth!
With all their millions, they'll have lived their whole lives
without ever knowing what fresh coffee was. Do you want
some butter? It's mine. Fresh from the churn. They have to
eat up yesterday's.

SEMINARIST [*ill at ease*]. I don't think I should ever have come
here.

MARIE JEANNE. More fool you then. You've a few weeks' holi-
day from the seminary before doing your army service, and
the chance of earning yourself a bit of money. That's a
postal order or two I shan't have to send you.

SEMINARIST. I never asked you for money.

MARIE JEANNE. What do you take me for? If my son wants to
have a quick smoke in the privy, or buy himself a little treat,
a fine thing if he couldn't afford it. Who is it cooks for you
over there? A priest?

SEMINARIST. No. A nun.

MARIE JEANNE [*snorting as she serves him*]. I can just see it!
Very tasty that must be. Have some marmalade. That's
what the rich have on their bread in the morning, orange

marmalade. They need it to keep going. It wears you out, doing nothing all day. [*She opens a pot.*] No. This one's overcooked. They can have that. I'll soon fatten you up, you great string bean!

SEMINARIST. What did you tell them?

MARIE JEANNE [*working away as she speaks; she never stops for a second*]. Not that you were my son, that's for sure. I'm no fool. When the Abbé who taught the children Latin told them he had to go home to nurse his sick brother, they started to panic. Just fancy, if those little darlings had poor-quality Latin rammed down their throats for those two months! Some unknown priest who didn't know how important they were and taught them pauper's Latin! Why, they'd carry the scar for the rest of their lives, poor loves! Everybody gave advice. Promised to write to all their friends. Baron Jules had just met the Papal Nuncio at a tea party, a piece of luck, that. Two weeks later they were still arguing over it and nothing had been settled. So one morning, when I took up my accounts, I said, "If your Ladyship is still looking for someone, there's the son of a rich lady down in my village. I've known him since he was a baby, he's just doing his third year in the seminary. . . ." Took a great weight off their minds, that did. [*She turns back to her stove.*] Only, it's like the coffee. They'll never know it's my old warmed-up brew they're drinking.

SEMINARIST [*indignantly*]. How could you! I don't want to stay here. It's all a lie!

MARIE JEANNE [*quizzing him, her eyes hard*]. How do you think life's lived, priest? How do you think one tears one's living out of other people? Over in your seminary—young and pure as you all are—do you always tell each other everything? Do you? And your beloved dormitory companion—the one who's so handsome and so rich, and who's chosen

God and poverty—did you tell him about me? [*The boy does not answer.*] Answer me! Your two black cassocks—are they the same?

SEMINARIST [*dully*]. Yes.

MARIE JEANNE. And your two beds—the same too? The little basin of cold water in the morning, is there just one between the two of you?

SEMINARIST. Yes.

MARIE JEANNE. And you've decided to serve our Lord's poor, both of you. But you did tell him, did you, that you were a servant's son?

SEMINARIST [*dully*]. No.

MARIE JEANNE. Then stop putting on airs. Snatch what you can snatch here before you go into the army, that's all. And don't be afraid. If we happen to meet in the morning when I take up my accounts, I'll call you Father Thomas. [ADELE, *the kitchen maid, comes in.* MARIE JEANNE *shouts.*] Oh, so you've decided to come down, have you? In the Old Girl's day, we were polishing the copper pans by six o'clock and at seven she'd ring for you to pick up a scrap of paper she'd tossed wide of her wastepaper basket when she was doing her correspondence after Mass. When she died, we killed three bottles of old burgundy in the servants' hall to celebrate, but I still take off my cap to her. With that woman you knew where you stood and you came downstairs on time.

ADELE [*in a murmur*]. I felt ill.

MARIE JEANNE. In the Old Girl's day, servants weren't ill. They knew that and because they knew it they didn't feel any the worse. Now skivvies have the vapors just like ladies. Must have their little tablets. And a doctor if their guts rumble.

ADELE. I'm not asking for anything.

MARIE JEANNE [*banging a bowl of coffee down on the table*].
Drink your coffee. That you're entitled to.

ADELE [*with a retch of disgust*]. I couldn't.

MARIE JEANNE. Milady feels queasy! Would Milady like us to
call a doctor? Since the new Countess there's one for us, all
arranged. Not the one they have upstairs, he's too expensive.
Another one, who's more of a vet. Shall I send the lad over
for him?

ADELE *gives a horrified shriek and clutches at her abdomen.*

ADELE. No! I don't want the doctor!

MARIE JEANNE [*looks at her penetratingly*]. You, my girl . . .
[*She pulls her toward her and gives her a hard, searching
look.*] All right. We'll talk about this later when we're alone.
Get down to your scrubbing and go and be sick if you feel
like it. Girls don't die of what you've got. [*A bell rings. She
goes to the indicator board.*] What's the matter with them
suddenly? Fallen out of their beds this morning? I expect
they want to know if you've arrived yet. Four days without
any Latin, the lambs! Come on. Say I served you your coffee
in the little parlor on the ground floor. From now on, that's
where you'll have it, your reverence. And the warmed-up
kind—like them. [*She jams her cap on her head.*] I always
put my cap on when I go up. It helps convince them that
they don't get hairs in their soup.

SEMINARIST [*following her with his suitcase*]. What are the
children like?

MARIE JEANNE [*as she goes*]. Cretins. Like all children.

*They have gone out without* ADELE *and the boy daring to look
at each other. When he goes, she runs to the door, half opens
it and looks after him. Then she takes off her shoes and, barefoot, begins to wash the kitchen floor.* MARCEL *comes in. He
watches as she swabs away with her behind stuck out.*

MARCEL [*softly*]. What a pretty little thing you are. I just don't understand you, Adele. Doing this dirty, heavy work when you could be serving dainty little drinks in a nice bar full of pretty lights down in Algiers. It's just silly.

ADELE [*dully, as she goes on scrubbing*]. I am silly.

MARCEL. That's nothing to boast about. Besides, it's not very nice for those who are taking so much trouble over you. I fancy you. I told you so. You don't fancy me—right! I never force a girl. We'll stay good friends. But I go to the trouble of talking about you to a mate of mine who knows the owner of a lovely bar out there, who happens to be looking for someone like you. We all have a drink one Sunday, to get acquainted. He's very polite, very proper. He tells you he thinks you'll do for the job and says he'll write to his friend. And now he's written, what happens? The answer's no! Well, how does it make me look? You have to consider other people a bit, you know.

ADELE. I'll pay for the stamp. I don't want to go to a country where I shan't know a single soul.

MARCEL. You soon make friends, it's easy! Besides, there are the other girls serving in the bar. You wouldn't be alone.

ADELE. I don't like new faces.

MARCEL. That's what *you* say! But do you think the old ones are much fun? Old man Romain, day in day out—Mother Joseph, Leon, Hugueline and me? Not to mention the up-stairs lot! Ha, if I was given the chance! . . . [*He looks at himself in his pocket mirror and pulls a face.*] I look ghastly. I worked myself to death again last night. The old man was at his club. She rang for me twice—on some pretext, as they say in the newspapers.

ADELE [*crying out*]. I don't want to know! I don't want to hear! Anyway, it isn't true! If it was, you wouldn't talk about it.

MARCEL. Why wouldn't I? Sleeping with the valet lowers you maybe, but sleeping with the mistress doesn't. Besides. [*He shows her a gold piece.*] If it wasn't true, where would I have got this, eh? You have to sweat for a whole month to earn a coin like that, my child. In that little Algiers bar I was telling you about, you'd make one of these every week, in tips alone. [*He raises a finger.*] More, if you know the ropes, I'm told. [*A pause; he adds carelessly.*] But there, you have to emigrate, dammit! [*He saunters out, humming. At the door he turns.*] We'll talk about it later. My friend says his friend will wait to hear from you before he engages any-one else. He's keen to have you, is that man. Young, good worker, not bad-looking, honest. He doesn't come across many like that, I don't suppose! From the point of view of the French out there, you're worth your weight in gold. [*He adds softly, cryptically.*] But, dammit, one has to emigrate. [*He goes out, up the upstage staircase.*]

*She goes on frenziedly scrubbing her floor. Young* ALEXIS *comes in with his vegetables, which he starts to peel.* ADELE *shouts at him.*

ADELE. Don't you go messing up my kitchen!

ALEXIS. I've got to do my potatoes, haven't I?

ADELE. Do them, then, but don't drop the peelings on the floor or you'll get my hand across your face.

ALEXIS. Hitting me, that's all you lot ever think about.

ADELE. You're the youngest. That's how *I* started. I was put out to work at twelve. I've had more clouts than lumps of meat, I can tell you.

ALEXIS. No, you're not like that. You're kind. When I was ill, you looked after me.

ADELE [*stonily*]. You're not ill now. And I don't earn enough to be kind. Get on with your work and don't dirty my kitchen if you care for the skin on your rump. When you're grown up you'll hit somebody smaller. That's justice. And it won't be you or I who'll change it.

*The boy goes on peeling in silence, squatting on his heels.*
Adele *wipes her floor.*
*The* Author *steps forward.*

Author. That wasn't such a bad beginning either. We had a glimpse of the old woman, and Adele and the young priest. Not to mention that little rat Marcel. Our nymphs and shepherds have become pimps and harlots. But Adele and the little priest, now that may turn out to be more difficult. You noticed the way they looked at each other, as if ashamed, not daring to look really. Already they could feel that there was going to be something between them. [*He watches her working away with a soft look in his eyes and murmurs.*] Adele! She is my sadness and my remorse. Everything that is about to happen to her I bear on my back like a burden of shame. Perhaps I should never have spoken to her. Perhaps I should never have opened her mind to certain things: it would have been simpler for her. . . . But it was to pay her a tribute which she would never have known in her wretchedness that I wanted to write this play. Unfortunately, there wasn't only her. All the characters are equally important in this story. [*For some time now, the* Superintendent *has been raising his hand like a schoolboy asking a question in class. The* Author *notices him.*] And there was the Superintendent fretting, wanting to have his say, too, anxious to go on with his enquiries. . . .

Superintendent. Can you blame me? To begin with, it's only human. And if you'd allow me to express an opinion . . .

Author [*rather discouraged by the turn things are taking*]. Go ahead. What can we lose?

Superintendent. I know you'll say I'm prejudiced, but the detective side is always popular, that's an undeniable fact.

I can't think why you're deliberately cutting it out. Not that
what you've been saying in general—about what you've felt
and haven't felt—isn't all quite valuable. It is. It's—shall I
say?—profound and poetic: in a sort of way. But what the
audience wants is suspense.

AUTHOR [*loftily*]. My good man, if you knew how profoundly
indifferent I am to suspense!

SUPERINTENDENT [*sententiously*]. You're making a big mistake.
Look at *Oedipus Rex*—there's plenty of it in that. And you
can't sniff at Euripides as a fellow dramatist, can you now?

AUTHOR [*very loftily*]. *Oedipus Rex* is by Sophocles. But how
on earth did you come to read that?

SUPERINTENDENT [*modestly*]. In a train. A girl left it behind on
the seat. [*He adds.*] Choice little piece she was, too. It makes
you wonder why she was reading that. A student, I suppose.
. . . Anyway, I only meant that it's owing to that—suspense,
I mean—that murder plays are always so sure-fire, even if
they're written in double dutch by a Serbian peasant. Good
God, man, there's a murder in your story, isn't there? Make
the most of it! I know the public, they're sitting there saying
to themselves—shall I say?—*sotto voce*, this is all very nice,
but just who *did* kill the cook?

*The* AUTHOR *has gone to sit in a corner.*

AUTHOR [*bored*]. That doesn't interest me much, I must say.
It's a detail.

SUPERINTENDENT. Murder is never a detail. Especially for the
victim. Anyway, between ourselves, who did kill the woman?

*The* AUTHOR *has clearly decided to wash his hands of the
whole thing. He lights a cigarette and says contemptuously:*

AUTHOR. Carry on, then, man, carry on! Do it yourself, since
you're so keen. Play your other scenes, go on. Ask your questions. Do your investigating. You might even find out who
did it. Then you can tell *me*.

SUPERINTENDENT. Right, I will! I'll go straight into the interrogation scene with the scullery boy.

AUTHOR [*very Pontius Pilate*]. Suit yourself. Question the lad,
do. It's a waste of time, but I wash my hands of it. I'm
telling you now, that's not the point of the play. [*To the
audience.*] He was a sweet lad, too, that scullery boy. There's
a character who would have been worth a little more attention. You'll see at the end of the play what he's there for.
Oh, don't worry, thanks to this lad, you'll have your glimmer
of hope at the end. [*He calls to* ADELE, *who is still scrubbing.*] Would you clear the stage for a moment, dear? He's
going to do his scene with the Superintendent. You've already left for Algiers by then. I'll call you back. [ADELE
*obediently wrings out her cloth, puts her bucket and mop
away, picks up her shoes and goes submissively out. The*
AUTHOR *watches her go and murmurs, moved.*] You see?—
she never says no. She obeys, that's all. She will obey to the
very end. [*To the* SUPERINTENDENT.] The stage is yours, my
dear fellow, but do get a move on so we can reach the heart
of the thing.

*The* SUPERINTENDENT *mimes his entrance into the kitchen.
The lights come on in the corner, where the scullery boy is
still peeling his potatoes.*

SUPERINTENDENT [*jovially*]. So Monday or Friday, morning or
evening, you still do your vegetables! They can murder
everyone in the house but you don't care; you just peel
away.

ALEXIS [*quite without bitterness*]. I've never done anything
else, ever since I've been here. You need a terrible lot of
potatoes for a big house. They're always saying to me,
"Haven't you finished yet, lazybones?" I'm not lazy. But,
with a potato, if you want to make the peelings thin, it
takes time. And I don't like botching a job.

SUPERINTENDENT. Once they're all mashed up, my boy . . .

ALEXIS [*quietly*]. It's nothing to do with me what they do with them afterward. I peel them the way they ought to be peeled and that's that. I can't see an eye in a potato.

SUPERINTENDENT. I see. You do it like an artist. You should have seen me in the army. I'd polish off my pile in ten minutes. [*He pulls a knife out of his pocket and squats beside the boy.*] Here. I'll give you a hand. I've got some time to spare this morning.

ALEXIS [*as they both peel away*]. What are you supposed to be doing here?

SUPERINTENDENT. Just this—wandering about, chatting. Learning things.

ALEXIS. Is that your job?

SUPERINTENDENT. Yes.

ALEXIS. It's a good job then. Not tiring.

SUPERINTENDENT. Don't you believe it. My brain works. And brainwork is the hardest.

ALEXIS. So they say. But I've never seen a brain sweat. [*He cries out.*] Here, you're wasting them! Look at what's left of that potato!

SUPERINTENDENT. That was standard size in the army. Big ones or little ones, they all turned out the same.

ALEXIS [*severely*]. You're not in the army now. If you can't work properly leave it alone and let me do it.

SUPERINTENDENT. Right, Sergeant! I'll peel this one as fine as cigarette paper for you. [*He peels away conscientiously.*] Tell me, you knew Adele, didn't you, when she was here?

ALEXIS. Yes, of course.

SUPERINTENDENT. What was she like?

ALEXIS. Fairhaired——

SUPERINTENDENT. No. I meant as a person. Was she a nice girl, kind?

ALEXIS. Yes.

SUPERINTENDENT. She had her little flings, I suppose, with the other fellows. [*The boy looks at him.*] I'm just saying that, of course, . . . I don't know.

ALEXIS. If you don't know, then don't say it. If you're going to say bad things about people then leave my potatoes alone.

SUPERINTENDENT. All right. Don't get cross. Don't you ever say bad things about people?

ALEXIS [*stonily*]. No.

SUPERINTENDENT. Yet I gather they don't spare you the wallopings. The Old Woman, the one who's dead, was she good to you?

ALEXIS [*woodenly*]. Yes.

SUPERINTENDENT. That's odd. I seem to remember hearing that you called her "the Old Cow." It was her whom you referred to, was it?

ALEXIS. She's dead now. And I never say anything against the dead.

SUPERINTENDENT. The dead are the living that were. A dead swine doesn't make a saint. And what about Leon the coachman? You aren't going to tell me he's a nice fellow? [*He shows him the potato.*] What do you think of this one, Sergeant?

ALEXIS [*gravely examining the potato*]. A bit better. But your hands aren't clean. And you can't fool a potato; if you haven't washed your hands it goes all gray like yours.

SUPERINTENDENT [*sheepishly*]. You can wash the potatoes afterward.

ALEXIS. You may as well wash your hands first.

SUPERINTENDENT. Right. I'll wash my hands then, Sergeant. [*He washes his hands at the sink and asks casually.*] Did you ever see them fight, Leon and old Marie Jeanne, I mean?

ALEXIS [*unforthcoming*]. Sometimes.

SUPERINTENDENT. They didn't care for each other much, eh?

ALEXIS. People can knock each other about and still care.

SUPERINTENDENT [*wiping his hands on his handkerchief*]. Yes, that's true enough. You know more than you appear to. And I'm sure if you cared to talk . . . Did Leon draw his knife sometimes? I'm told he used to like frightening people with it. [*He produces his flick knife.*]

ALEXIS [*coolly*]. Those knives are illegal; never mind, we'll overlook it this time. Now just you see if you can't do me a good dozen—nice and fine—while I fetch up my carrots and turnips from the cellar. Let's see what you're good for, you and all your swank.

*He goes out, leaving the* SUPERINTENDENT *looking rather crestfallen. He goes on disconsolately peeling potatoes. Enter* HUGUELINE *with a tray she has brought down from upstairs.*

HUGUELINE. Oh, I beg your pardon, sir! I didn't know you were down here. In the kitchen!

SUPERINTENDENT [*rising in confusion*]. Nor did I. I mean, I was just passing. I saw these potatoes. I adore peeling potatoes! A whim of mine. I just couldn't stop myself. Silly, isn't it? [*He laughs fatuously.*]

HUGUELINE [*simpering*]. You couldn't stop yourself yesterday either. Very ill-bred it is, the way you carry on, do you know that?

SUPERINTENDENT. Get along with you! I had some questions to put to you—shall I say?—professionally.

HUGUELINE [*provocatively*]. Oh, yes. We start by putting questions and we end up by putting our hands here, there, and everywhere. I don't like that sort of thing, I don't like it at all.

SUPERINTENDENT [*drawing closer*]. I can't somehow believe that, my pretty. We've experience of women in the force. Baron Jules keeps his hands to himself, eh, and I don't suppose?

HUGUELINE. He's the master's son, that's different.

SUPERINTENDENT. It's a bit—shall I say?—feudal, don't you think—that argument?

HUGUELINE [*slyly*]. Besides, he's very generous.

SUPERINTENDENT [*a little dashed*]. I'm working at the moment, you know, my lass. And expenses are extremely meager in the force. If I wanted to be—shall I say?—a stickler for duty, I could pester quite a lot of people here. A hearty little interrogation in true police style, that's never much fun. Whereas a friendly little chat——

HUGUELINE [*worried*]. Look here, I haven't done anything!

SUPERINTENDENT. You can never be sure, can you? Besides, you'd have to prove it, my child. And proving you haven't done anything—when you haven't—is even harder than when you *have*. [*He moves nearer to her.*] Do you see what I'm driving at, my pretty?

HUGUELINE [*defeated*]. And I should have thought you were a nice man.

SUPERINTENDENT [*softly*]. That doesn't mean anything in the police force. [*He takes her in his arms.*] Tell me, my heart, the Count . . . I'm told he was—shall I say?—on the best of terms with the deceased at one time. Is that true? [HUGUELINE *bursts out laughing. He adds, vexed.*] What are you laughing at?

HUGUELINE. The deceased! The things you call people! Anyway, I wasn't even born at that time.

SUPERINTENDENT. Since you've been here—have you ever seen them?

HUGUELINE. You're joking, aren't you? His Grace could aim higher than that.

SUPERINTENDENT [*slyly*]. With you?

HUGUELINE [*a little disappointedly*]. Oh, no. He never had any dealings of that kind with the staff.

SUPERINTENDENT. Tell me, the little priest—is it true nobody knew who he was?

HUGUELINE. I never bothered with him much. In the first place, cassocks . . . The thought that there's a man underneath—it's not that I'm a prude, but it puts me off.

SUPERINTENDENT [*pawing her absent-mindedly*]. And Adele, did it put her off too?

HUGUELINE. That idiot! Mind you, he wasn't a real priest. He hadn't properly said yes yet.

AUTHOR [*leaping up in exasperation*]. No, no, no! That won't bring my play any further forward. Get it into your head once and for all that Adele is already in North Africa and the seminarist ran away, immediately after the stabbing.

SUPERINTENDENT [*needled*]. At least I'm sticking to the point.

AUTHOR. What point?

SUPERINTENDENT. Who killed the cook?

AUTHOR [*determinedly*]. Right. Now I shall use my authority. Who is the author of this play—you or I?

SUPERINTENDENT [*astutely*]. What play? We haven't got one yet.

AUTHOR. My good man. One quick telephone call to police headquarters and they'll send me another inspector.

SUPERINTENDENT. That would be against all the rules of dramatic construction.

AUTHOR. At this stage in the game that's the least of my worries, I can promise you. What I want to do now is to bring Adele and the seminarist together, the first time they told each other that they were in love. [*He goes out into the wings and brings back the two young people.*] Come along, you two. Where did it take place?

ADELE. What?

AUTHOR. Your love scene.

ADELE [*crying out*]. But we never had a love scene, ever! You mustn't make everybody think that, you mustn't!

AUTHOR. Where did your first conversation take place then, if you prefer it. In the kitchen?

ADELE. Yes.

AUTHOR. You went downstairs hoping to see her, did you?

SEMINARIST [*shamefaced*]. Yes. That is . . . I went down to ask for some lime tea. I'd caught a chill and I didn't like ringing the bells for my personal needs. But I *was* hoping to meet her, yes. . . .

AUTHOR [*to* ADELE, *who has started to take off her shoes*]. What are you doing? We're going to start your scene.

ADELE [*quietly*]. I'm taking off my shoes. I was washing the floor that time too. . . . One was forever having to scrub out that kitchen. And it was because I was barefoot that I felt—— [*She suddenly bursts out.*] Oh, it's too ugly! It's too ugly! You've no right to keep on talking about it. It's mine, all of that. It's my secret. And I'm too ashamed. It's almost as if he was a priest, don't you see, with those robes of his. And last night again, that other one came up to my room. I'd locked the door but he forced it open with his knife and I didn't dare scream because of the others. I'd rather agree right away about going to Algiers! At least I won't be a burden to anybody anymore.

AUTHOR [*in despair*]. What a mentality! What can you do with characters like that? Can't you see what you're saying is absolutely stupid? It's a sloppy, sludgy mess! [*Exploding.*] It's pseudo-Chekhov! They'll never accept a character like that!

ADELE [*dazed*]. I don't understand what you're saying, but I do know that it's the simplest thing to do.

AUTHOR [*yelling with exasperation*]. What is?

ADELE [*going back into her shell*]. If you shout I shan't say anything. Everybody always shouts when they talk to me. Just order me to do something and I'll do it. I know how to obey. But there's no point in shouting.

AUTHOR [*more gently*]. But there's no question of ordering you, my dear. Now come, answer me quietly and calmly. What is the simplest thing for you to do, Adele, my child?

ADELE. Going where I have to go.

AUTHOR. But, good God, you aren't a complete innocent! You must have realized by now—anyway the others have told you—just where Marcel wants to send you?

ADELE [*woodenly*]. Yes.

AUTHOR. Then you're arguing like a child. Why say it's the simplest thing to do?

ADELE. Because then everybody will be satisfied and they won't keep on at me any more.

AUTHOR [*gently*]. Who keeps on at you? [*Sighing.*] I'm so sorry!

ADELE. Everybody. Marie Jeanne, who's tumbled to it that her son's hanging round me. [*She indicates the* SEMINARIST *with a regretful little gesture.*] And him, who's always telling me I must stay pure. That other one, who keeps pestering me to go with him again and who knocks me about. And then there's Marcel, who keeps saying he's gone to a lot of trouble and how they've bought the ticket and it's not right to say I won't go now. [*She adds with dignity.*] I am what I am but I've never cheated anybody. And the ticket alone is too expensive for me to pay back, never mind anything else. It would take me a year nearly and they say they can't wait a year—there's the interest on the money and that would make it even more.

AUTHOR [*very patiently*]. That's an absurd way to talk. No-body can force you to go to that bar in Algiers if you don't want. Even if they have already paid the fare.

SUPERINTENDENT. In the first place, they can get a refund on the ticket.

AUTHOR [*snapping at him*]. Be quiet! You're not here! Adele, listen to me. The Countess is a very kindhearted woman.

You must ask to see her and tell her all about it. Tell her
what's happened to you. She'll do something about it. She'll
protect you.

ADELE [*horrified*]. Oh, no! Never!

AUTHOR. Why not?

ADELE. I'd be too ashamed. Why, if she knew I was pregnant,
even! No, no, I'd rather go out to Algiers right away. It's
simpler.

SUPERINTENDENT [*stepping forward*]. I have an idea. I already
have a file on Marcel. Now, she comes and makes a com-
plaint. I listen to her, very humane, very understanding.
Short scene. Quickfire interrogation. I guess the whole story.
Police protection.

AUTHOR [*shrugging irritably*]. No, no, no, no! I tell you she's
already left for Algiers when you come to the house.

SUPERINTENDENT. I telephone immediately to the port authori-
ties at Marseilles.

AUTHOR [*exasperated*]. She's in Algiers, I tell you!

SUPERINTENDENT. A rogatory commission in Algiers!

AUTHOR. If you think they're going to all that trouble over a
servant girl who's been led astray! There are a dozen a day!

SUPERINTENDENT. But we have influence. . . . His Grace's
name, your own . . . you're becoming quite famous in
police circles, with all the successes you've had. They aren't
the traditional flatfoots these days, you know. [*The* AUTHOR
*takes his arm, exasperated, and leads him out into the
wings.*]

AUTHOR. You'll be doing me a favor if you'll just go and sit
down quietly with the others and wait for me, will you do
that? [*He comes back grunting; to the other two, who are
standing facing each other, embarrassed.*] I wish I'd never
invented that man. Let's be methodical, my dears, or we'll
never sort this out. Just say exactly what you said to each
other that evening. It was late. Everybody had gone up to

bed. She was finishing her floor, as usual. You, lad, you've come downstairs to ask her for some lime tea. Off you go. You, wash the floor. Right. A moment of silence and then he comes on.

*He withdraws. The* SEMINARIST *appears on the upstage staircase.*

SEMINARIST. Excuse me, Mademoiselle———

ADELE *brushes back a wisp of hair from her eyes with her bare arm and murmurs:*

ADELE. I'm doing the floor. [*She sees his eyes on her bare feet. She blushes and puts them awkwardly one on top of the other, as if ashamed.*] I work barefoot. It's easier. You don't leave so many marks. It must look funny in the city. They're country ways. I'm from the country.

SEMINARIST [*softly*]. So am I. [*An awkward pause.*] I came down to see if I couldn't have some lime tea. I think I've caught a chill.

ADELE. You should have rung for it.

SEMINARIST. Oh no, I wouldn't have dared disturb anyone, not for my own needs. Besides, it's late. I was working for my October examinations. I shouldn't want to disturb———

ADELE. I'll get you some tea.

SEMINARIST. You're working very late, too, aren't you?

ADELE. I've got to wash the kitchen floor every night. So I have to wait until everybody has gone up, otherwise they make it dirty again. Sometimes they stay up late, talking. It's natural . . . When the day's done, you like to sit and chat. . . .

SEMINARIST. Yet you're first down in the morning.

ADELE [*softly, with a smile*]. I have to light the fire.

SEMINARIST. It's hard in the winter, having to be up first.

ADELE. A little. When you're looking for the matches and you light the lamp that smells of cold. And then, when

the sticks begin to crackle in the stove, there's a moment
when you feel good. You're almost afraid that the others
will wake up. When the others come down, it means the
day's started. [*She adds, kindly.*] In the seminary, I expect
they make you get up early, too.

SEMINARIST. Yes. It's still dark.

ADELE. Do you light your own fire?

SEMINARIST. We don't have a fire.

ADELE. It must be even drearier for you than it is for me,
then. [*She is by the stove. She turns with a timorous little
smile.*] Is that wrong, what I said?

SEMINARIST. Why?

ADELE. Because with you, as it's for our Lord, it must seem
easier. . . .

SEMINARIST [*smiling*]. Oh, we aren't heroes, you know. You
still feel sick and dizzy, being up so early. So long as you
haven't had your hunk of bread and your mug of coffee.

ADELE [*smiling*]. I hope it's good coffee?

SEMINARIST [*smiling too*]. Well, good black water.

ADELE [*suddenly very young and sweet, almost despite herself*]. It's a pity they don't have girls to wait on you. I'd
make you some, hot and strong. [*She has made the infusion.
She holds out the cup and asks anxiously.*] Was that disrespectful of me, saying that?

SEMINARIST [*flushing crimson*]. No. Why?

ADELE [*looking at him, a little emboldened*]. You can never
tell with a—— [*She breaks off and asks.*] You're very young.
Do they take priests as young as that?

SEMINARIST [*smiling*]. We aren't priests yet. We're just learning. We haven't taken our vows yet. To be a priest you have
to be worthy. It takes a long time.

ADELE. When will you be a priest?

SEMINARIST. At the end of next year if I pass my final exams.

ADELE. And are there some who don't go on to the end?

SEMINARIST. Yes. Those who aren't sure.

ADELE. What do they do?

SEMINARIST. They go home. But it's hard being a village boy again. People resent them. The priest tells everybody they've stolen money from the Church. [*He adds dully.*] And the girls jeer at them.

ADELE. Oh, girls are silly. Perhaps they don't feel so much like jeering really. Besides, if there's one who loves him . . . she doesn't jeer.

SEMINARIST [*quietly*]. Yes, but then she's afraid the others will jeer at her, and she never dares to marry him. In those little villages, you know, it's . . . It would have to be someone with a lot of courage. Or else they'd have to go away somewhere to work. But that's not always easy; the girl's parents won't let her. [*He hands back the cup.*] Here's the cup. Thank you.

ADELE [*kindly*]. Did it warm you up?

SEMINARIST. Yes.

*A pause.*

ADELE [*embarrassed suddenly*]. Now I'm going to put the lights out and we must say good night. Perhaps it might be best if you went up first.

SEMINARIST. Yes, of course. Excuse me . . . We might not have another chance to see each other alone and I only wanted to tell you that . . . I can see they aren't very kind to you here, not even—— [*He hesitates and then says.*] not even Madame Marie Jeanne.

ADELE [*with a little gesture*]. It's always like that when you work.

SEMINARIST. She spoke to you very roughly yesterday and I wanted to say it made me feel ashamed. And ashamed that she's—you know it—my mother. And so I wanted to say I was sorry.

ADELE [*horrified*]. You mustn't talk like that! [*She has turned out the lamps. She says softly.*] There. The lights are out. We must go upstairs now.

SEMINARIST [*in the dark*]. Yes. [*A pause.*] I know you're unhappy. I shall pray for you. . . . [ *A pause; he adds.*] Only I'm not sure that I can pray very well anymore. I try hard. I do everything I can.

ADELE [*softly, tenderly almost*]. Why did you go there then?

SEMINARIST [*dully*]. I was afraid of being a peasant.

*Another pause.*

ADELE. You must go up now. . . . Somebody might come in.

SEMINARIST. Yes.

*He disappears as if reluctant. ADELE listens as he goes up. Then she notices the cup. She washes, wipes, and puts it away. She throws a little black shawl over her shoulders, puts her shoes on, and is about to go upstairs with her lamp when the*
AUTHOR *asks gently:*

AUTHOR. Is that all you said to each other that evening?

ADELE. Yes, sir.

AUTHOR. Right. You can go, my dear. Good night.

[*She goes out.*
*He comes back on stage, in despair.*

Where does that scene lead, I ask you? Nowhere. They're in love, yes, that's quite obvious, but they'll never get to the point of saying so. They're too bashful, both of them. They're paralyzed. That child has been sodden with shame ever since she was little. And that other great booby, swallowing his Adam's apple, wiping his clammy great hands—they're hopeless characters! Hopeless! Good God Almighty.

There's got to be a love scene, dammit, in this play! [*The other characters from above stairs have started to appear shyly as if coming for news. The* AUTHOR *sees them and shouts.*] And there are the others upstairs who haven't said a word yet! Baron Jules, the Count's son from his first marriage, and his wife the Baroness—charming characters— the Countess, the children. [*Raising his arms in exasperation.*] Children! What possessed me to bring children into this? . . . [*The downstairs characters have begun to invade the stage, too.*] And there's old Romain, the butler, to whom I'd promised a comedy scene! And Marie Jeanne. She was supposed to be a huge character, a sort of female Falstaff. [*He shouts suddenly like a maniac.*] Not a scrap of talent! Not a scrap! I shall have to start working in films! Or journalism! Anything! Why, I'd rather be a critic! That's it! I'll look for the flaws in other people's plays. But not in my own! Not in my own! Not any more, dear God, not any more!

*All the characters watch this fit in dismay. The* SUPERINTEND-ENT, *who has come back looking pretty satisfied with the turn events have taken, says to him, heaping coals on the fire:*

SUPERINTENDENT. Not to mention the audience, who are still sitting there wondering who killed the cook. . . .

*The* AUTHOR *has dropped into a chair, defeated, in the center of the stage, surrounded by his characters. He asks, almost humbly:*

AUTHOR. Well, what's to be done, then?

SUPERINTENDENT [*smiling*]. An intermission.

*The* AUTHOR *leaps to his feet, a good ten years younger.*

AUTHOR. An intermission! It will give us time to think. [*He steps forward to the audience and announces.*] An intermis-

sion. I expect you need one too. [*Shouting up to the flies.*]
Curtain!

As the curtain falls, he adds:

Don't run away, though, will you?

*The Curtain Is Down.*

# ACT TWO

*Same set. When the curtain goes up all the characters are on stage, either in the kitchen or on the stairs. The gentry are on one side, the servants on the other. The rise of the curtain seems to surprise them somewhat and they say nothing at first. They exchange anxious glances and look into the wings as if they were expecting someone. Eventually* ROMAIN, *the butler, shrugs fatalistically, clears his throat, and begins.*

ROMAIN. Good masters they were, too. A settled life. Order. And then, one day . . .

LEON [*somber, in his corner, pouring himself a glass of red wine from the bottle which has remained on the table*]. Good masters, there's no such thing. I remember in the Old Girl's day . . .

ROMAIN. She was hard, but she was a lady. A true lady. Such as you don't see any more.

LEON [*growling*]. A lady. Two horses to harness of a morning for six o'clock Mass, winter and summer alike. If you've got religion under your skin, you go on bleeding foot. You don't muck up the coachman.

ROMAIN [*with great dignity*]. You will kindly use different language when you speak to me, M. Leon. I run this household, and you owe me, to some extent, the shadow of respect which you owe to your masters.

LEON [*muttering*]. The shadow of respect of my ass.

ROMAIN. There is an established social order. For my part, it satisfies me. I consider that every man finds his true dignity in his rightful place.

43

LEON. The dignity of my ass. We don't have any dignity, not our sort, and we've no call to have, either.

ROMAIN. I have always discerned a deplorable attitude in you —and in that unfortunate Marie Jeanne, too, for that matter —quite deplorable. And had it rested with me, I've never left you in any doubt that——

LEON [*sneering*]. But it rested with Marie Jeanne's titties that his Grace treated himself to for five years. After that, she moved down to the kitchen. [*He lifts a finger.*] For life!

ROMAIN [*riled*]. I have never wished to know. Above stairs is above stairs. What goes on is their affair. In my position you have to learn to keep your eyes shut.

LEON. *You* have! Me, when someone has done something to me I have to take it out on someone else. The nags in the stables—it's them I took it out on, once the doors were good and bolted. Till I drew blood. Beasts costing two thousand louis apiece; they're worth ten times as much as the coachman. I taught them to be thoroughbreds, the bitches!

ROMAIN [*raising his hands in despair*]. There was a good scheme of things, though. It may have been good, it may have been bad, but it was order. And now—— [*He yelps suddenly.*] I've never countenanced disorder! We must all rally round her Grace, the second Countess, who is a saint, and help her to forget these sad events.

LEON [*cackling*]. A saint? The Sugarplum? Hey, Marcel?

MARCEL [*evasively*]. Yes, well . . . I used to make out that she . . . But it wasn't true. I may as well admit it now. She never rang for me at night when the old fellow was at his club. I just said that to make myself sound important.

*The* COACHMAN *looks at him, then heaves a sigh of disappointment and helps himself to another drink.*

LEON. Oh. Pity. That's the only thing about her that didn't put me off too much—her being one for bed.

HUGUELINE. She wasn't a bad soul, you couldn't say that. It was her way of being good that got on your nerves. Marrying the old man—more than twenty years older than her—and not deceiving him, well, I ask you!

ROMAIN [*screeching*]. Her Grace belongs to a world where virtue is a tradition!

HUGUELINE. Give me Baroness Jules any day. She was easy to get on with, she was. A slipper at your head every so often, when she had her nervous spells, but that's all. And never wore her dresses above three times. Pity my behind was so much fuller than hers. That's where they always split. But the full evening rig and a party every night. And a new lover every season. That's class!

ROMAIN [*conceding, tightlipped*]. Her Ladyship Baroness Jules has her traditions too. They were different traditions, that's all. The aristocratic world has diverse traditions which we must respect without understanding.

MARCEL [*grudgingly*]. Baron Jules was somebody, too. Chorus girls, of course, and his own table at Maxim's and his special brandy and all the rest of it, but that didn't count, not really. With him, it was racing. Every day, two hours poring over the list of starters, pen in hand. And he'd pass on all his tips. Only, where he bet ten louis, I'd bet one franc. Which explains why I always stayed a menial. Without capital behind you in the modern world, you get nowhere.

BARON JULES, *who is sitting nonchalantly on the stairs with his arm in a sling, comes to life and says to the* BARONESS, *who is sitting beside him:*

BARON JULES. These enquiries are going to be most disagreeable, there's no getting away from it. We really can't be held responsible for everything that goes on in our own kitchens. The fact remains that the very next day everybody had the paper open at the crime page. I must admit I had a certain success at the club. "What's this, Jules? We all know you kept a good table, but did you have to send your cook to larder?" I came near to being a laughing stock. In the end I had to toss the glove at des Epinglettes. And that imbecile, who could never handle a penknife let alone a sword, slips on the wet ground and contrives to cut me in the shoulder, which is charming just before the Deauville season, with the golf and the pigeon shooting. All I have left is baccarat, where I can still draw with my left hand. This summer is going to ruin me. Quite positively.

BARONESS. And what about me? Do you think it's going to be fun? The story grew and grew until now everyone is saying you fought a duel over your cook! I shan't dare show my face. Positively! [*She says the word exactly as he did: it is clearly the expression of the day. She exclaims.*] My dear, you forget we're due for luncheon at the Austrian Embassy. You'll never be ready. You need twice as much time as I do.

BARON JULES. I'm not going. I warned Coco that you'd be coming alone. With my arm in a sling I shall positively not be able to eat a thing. And I couldn't decently ask my neighbor to help me cut up my meat—she's sure to be a hundred with a double coronet—I know Coco's luncheons! I shall lunch at Maxim's.

BARONESS [*lightly*]. And you'll have someone there, will you, of the right age to assist you?

BARON JULES. Certainly.

BARONESS. That's perfect then. I shall send the coachman over to Zizi's, who is going to Coco's, too, and ask him to come and fetch me. He'll be delighted to take your place.

BARON JULES [*blithely*]. He's used to it. Positively.

BARONESS. Please don't be witty, it's still very early.

*The* COUNTESS *comes to life and murmurs:*

COUNTESS. Little Adele . . . I was very fond of her. . . . Her humility moved me to tears sometimes. I meant it to be such a gift when I asked her to be Thibaut's godmother. The things she screamed at us! With those dirty words, on purpose! You could feel she was screaming them on purpose, like incantations. I shall never forget her eyes. I'd come to give her everything, and all I got from her was hatred.

COUNT [*quietly*]. I told you you should never go below stairs. Each of us must play his role where Fate has placed him. Fate has placed you in the drawing rooms of the first floor. When you need something, my dear, ring the bell. They will come up. But don't ever concern yourself with what happens below stairs. When one leans over and has a look —it always leads to trouble. I found that out. Justice is God's affair. We must let Heaven shoulder its own responsibilities. You'll excuse me, my dear, but I promised Mme. de Merteuil I'd ride with her this morning. She has a new mount she isn't very sure of. Do you believe in this fad for riding anglo-arabs? It's pure affectation. At the first serious obstacle she'll have trouble. I'm sure of it.

COUNTESS. I admire your levity. I can't think of anything but this tragedy. [*She turns to look at the young* SEMINARIST, *who is standing upstage, motionless.*] Yet he was very sweet, that little priest, when he arrived that first day. . . .

COUNT [*who has turned around, too*]. Very sweet. The image of myself at twenty. Except for his hands, which were bigger than mine. . . .

COUNTESS [*with reproachful sadness*]. Thibaut——

COUNT. My dear, what's the sense in making a mystery of it? Within a week it will be in all the papers.

COUNTESS [*hurt*]. Don't laugh. You make a joke of everything. You loved that . . . [*She falters.*]

COUNT [*turning to her*]. That . . . ?

COUNTESS. I don't know what word to use, quite. . . .

COUNT [*icy, suddenly*]. There are several in the time-honored terminology. That woman, that slut, that servant?

COUNTESS [*gently*]. I don't want to say anything hurtful, Thibaut.

COUNT [*almost aggressively*]. It's difficult not to. All the words are. Believe me, we'd do better not to talk about all this, my dear. The subject borders on the odious or the grotesque. And what is more, it's a topic on which I find I'm very sensitive. It would be most gracious of you not to refer to it again.

COUNTESS [*gently*]. You went down yourself, though?

COUNT [*deliberately uncomprehending*]. Down where?

COUNTESS. Below stairs.

COUNT [*evasively*]. Once. It was so long ago. And it no longer concerns anyone but that middle-aged lady up there in her picture frame, who has the good taste to be dead at this particular moment.

COUNTESS [*after a pause*]. How hard you can be, Thibaut. You who are so kind. I should like to hear you cry out, just once.

COUNT [*tersely*]. I trust you never will. I leave that to animals and to the rabidly emotional, who incidentally have much in common. Man has the good fortune to possess an articulate language and a code, which allows him to express the shades of meaning of his mind, and—if he absolutely must —his heart. He doesn't have to cry out. [*One feels suddenly that his courtesy is being somewhat sorely tried. He adds testily.*] Have you quite simply devised this scheme to oblige me to keep Mme. de Merteuil waiting?

COUNTESS [*smiling with sudden lightness*]. Far from my thoughts any such dark designs! I was merely trying to reach —by this chance meeting—a husband who's at times unreachable.

*The* ELDER BOY *comes to life and asks:*

ELDER BOY. Mamma, who's to hear us our Latin verbs?

COUNTESS. I shall, of course. Have you your books?

ELDER BOY. Yes, Mamma. Will you be able to?

COUNTESS. Yes, perfectly well.

ELDER BOY [*impishly*]. Then why didn't you do it in the first place? You're much nicer than a priest. You smell good.

COUNTESS [*hiding a faint embarrassment*]. Why, because I have other duties in this house and I shouldn't have had time.

*The* YOUNGER BOY *comes to life.*

YOUNGER BOY. Will we have another priest?

COUNTESS. Of course.

ELDER BOY. Did that last one have an elder brother who was ill as well?

COUNTESS. No. He was called away suddenly, too, but for a different reason.

ELDER BOY. What reason, Mamma?

COUNTESS. You're too inquisitive. A telegram.

ELDER BOY. Is it true that Cook's dead?

YOUNGER BOY. Marcel told us she'd been killed. Is it true?

COUNTESS. Marcel is a ninny. And I've forbidden you to talk to the servants all the time. [*She turns to* MARIE JEANNE *who has been standing motionless amongst the others since the beginning, as if she were miles away. Everyone looks at her.*] Marie Jeanne has been very ill and they've taken her to the hospital. But I expect she'll get well again, and if our Lord didn't mean her to get well, then she'd go to Heaven.

YOUNGER BOY. Will she be a cook in Heaven?

ELDER BOY. And Adele, Mamma, is it true Adele's gone away to live with black men? Is it true that it's so hot out there that she's going to work in her shift?

COUNTESS [*not grasping this at first*]. Why in her shift?

YOUNGER BOY [*repeating it*]. Why in her shift, Mamma?

COUNTESS [*understands suddenly and exclaims.*] My little boys are too inquisitive by far. Will you get it into your heads that you must not ask questions about things which don't concern you, or listen to nasty stories in the servants' hall. There's nothing so ill-bred.

*The* AUTHOR, *who has come in down below with the* SUPER-INTENDENT, *gives a start at the* COUNTESS' *last words.*

AUTHOR. What nasty stories? What's ill-bred? What is she talking about up there? [*He upbraids her.*] What are you talking about, Madame? And who gave you leave to speak anyway? It's outrageous! I go out for a coffee in the inter-mission, I come back—and they're speaking!

*Old* ROMAIN *has appeared down below.*

ROMAIN. I do apologize, sir. You mustn't hold it against us. It was I who started to speak on my own initiative, sir. They'd taken the curtain up—accidentally, no doubt—and we had to do something. So we took the liberty of continu-ing your play, sir.

AUTHOR [*appalled*]. By yourselves?

ROMAIN [*modestly*]. Yes, sir, with the means to hand. But you mustn't worry, sir, we didn't say anything vital. Chatter, that's all. We wouldn't have taken the liberty, sir.

AUTHOR [*in an anxious aside*]. But did they listen?

ROMAIN. Fairly well, sir, yes.

AUTHOR. Without coughing?

ROMAIN. Not too much. [*He adds.*] A little, though, I must say.

AUTHOR. I see. It can't have been too marvelous. [*He steps down to the audience.*] Excuse me, ladies and gentlemen. We shall now go on with the play proper. Clear the stage

please. [*Old* ROMAIN *has discreetly wandered away. The*
AUTHOR *calls him back.*] One second, my friend.

ROMAIN. Sir?

AUTHOR. You're a familiar character?

ROMAIN. Very good of you to remember, sir. I've been in use
for many years. *Traveler Without Luggage,* 1937, *Time Re-*
*membered,* 1940, *Dinner with the Family,* 1941, *Ring Round*
*the Moon,* 1947. You've always been most satisfied with my
services, sir. You even lent me to Mr. Oscar Wilde once,
sir, on the occasion of an adaptation on which you col-
laborated, sir.

AUTHOR [*modestly*]. I rather think it was Mr. Oscar Wilde
who lent you to me, originally. But never mind that. I should
like to ask you a question. A question which has a certain
importance for the Superintendent here, for his Lordship,
and for me, too. Is this a good establishment?

ROMAIN. Perfect, sir.

AUTHOR. And the staff?

ROMAIN [*with an evasive gesture*]. There's always room for
improvement. But on the whole, the persons employed here
are of a satisfactory moral and professional standard.

AUTHOR. The running of this little world must give you a fair
amount of worry, though?

ROMAIN. Since you do me the honor of asking, sir, I shall take
the liberty of confessing that things are not always as I might
wish. The chambermaid, for instance, is a fairly personable
young woman, but her tea-trays are not always all they might
be. She has no napkin instinct. Her lemon slices for after-
noon tea are frequently arranged without artistry. Once she
even forgot the sugar tongs. Admittedly it was a tray for his
Lordship Baron Jules, who always takes the sugar with his
fingers, but even so! It's a professional shortcoming which
would have the gravest consequences in the establishment

of the Duchess Dupont-Dufort. Here the tendency is to turn
a blind eye. If I may take the liberty of expressing an
opinion, sir, her Grace the Countess is too goodnatured.

AUTHOR. I'm told she used to be very concerned about the
well-being of her servants. Is it true that she even conceived
the plan of having the humblest one amongst you as godmother to her new baby? The scullery maid, the one who
disappeared.

ROMAIN [suddenly clamlike]. That was a regrettable episode,
which nearly ruined my career. I would prefer not to talk
about it. But it is true that there's a fashion nowadays for
a certain "social consciousness," for which the servants' hall
is not in the least grateful and which leads to a general
slackening off.

AUTHOR. You've noticed this, have you?

ROMAIN. With regret, sir, yes I have. In my day when the
masters went out, a part of the staff waited up. His Grace
might need a nightcap. Madame had to be undressed. And
in any case, there were the last orders to be taken. There
might be a change of plan for the following day. Nowadays,
there's a little note left in the kitchen somewhere, and
lucky you are if you even find it. These little instances of
laxness are bewildering to the staff.

AUTHOR. But the staff like their share of sleep like everyone
else, don't they?

ROMAIN. A little more rest and comfort is a secondary con-
sideration, sir. Look at Louis XV. I read in a booklet of
popular history that he had a trapdoor built, through which
a table came up ready set from the kitchens so that he
could dine quietly with her Grace the Countess du Barry.
The Revolution was at the gates. From that moment on,
monarchy was a lost cause. The King had the pleasure of
chopping up his own chicken and seventeen years later, to
the day, they were chopping off his grandson's head.

AUTHOR. I see you have a great political sense. Thank you, my good man.

ROMAIN. At your service, sir.                    [*He goes out.*

SUPERINTENDENT. He's frightening, that old fossil. It may be he who killed the cook, for carving the leg of lamb against the grain.

AUTHOR. My dear man, I've put up with your schoolboy jokes because I had to woo the audience at all costs. But the audience have had enough of appetizers now. They want to move on to the main dish. They'd like to know why exactly I've got them to come here.

SUPERINTENDENT [*with a disrespectful titter*]. So would you, I should think.

AUTHOR. Don't be insolent. Just because I wasn't able to write this play doesn't mean I don't know what it's meant to be about! As a rule, the plays you can't manage to write are just the ones where you have most to say. The moment you have more than three ideas in the theatre, you get into a muddle.

SUPERINTENDENT [*more and more disrespectful*]. Oh, quite. Look at Shakespeare.

AUTHOR [*cut to the quick*]. Shakespeare did as he liked! He probably never wrote the plays anyway! There were probably several of them at it! I could be Shakespeare, too, in those conditions.

SUPERINTENDENT. Well, would you like me to help you?

AUTHOR [*haughtily*]. My dear man, you're quite amusing in an opening scene, to take the chill off, but I won't create great drama with someone of your sort. You're a cardboard character, a relic of the old-time potboilers!

SUPERINTENDENT [*nettled*]. If that's your attitude . . .

AUTHOR [*mollified*]. You should never utter Shakespeare's name to a playwright; it's very hurtful.

*Voices are heard suddenly from the scullery.* MARIE JEANNE *has come in, dragging* ADELE *roughly by the arm. The* AUTHOR *and the* SUPERINTENDENT *make a few ineffectual moves to intervene and then retreat off the stage.*

MARIE JEANNE. You'll talk! You'll talk, you little slut! I've seen you whispering, the pair of you. That's the second time I've caught you at it. What was he saying to you?

ADELE. Nothing, I tell you! He wanted some polish for his boots.

MARIE JEANNE. He can put them out with the children's. They'll be polished for him.

ADELE [*quickly*]. I already offered to do them, he won't let me.

MARIE JEANNE [*eyeing her coldly*]. You offered to clean his boots?

ADELE. Yes. He won't let me.

MARIE JEANNE. It's your job to clean the boots now, is it? I thought Marcel and Hugueline took care of that.

ADELE. I thought it might be less awkward for him if I did it. He's always grubby and untidy. Nobody looks after him. There are I don't know how many buttons missing on his cassock.

MARIE JEANNE. And you offered to sew them on for him, no doubt?

ADELE. Yes. [*She cries suddenly.*] You're his mother! Why don't you do it, instead of leaving him like that? If I had a son, if I had somebody of my own to look after . . .

MARIE JEANNE [*softly*]. You'd be a good little wife, wouldn't you? You'd wait for him meekly in your kitchen all day, preparing tasty little dishes for him. And in the evening, when he came back from work, you'd stand behind his chair and wait on him and watch him while he ate. And if he said he'd enjoyed his supper, you'd feel a great warm bubble of bliss bursting inside you. You'd have fed your fill.

ADELE [*softly, her eyes closed*]. Yes.

MARIE JEANNE *looks at her a moment, with hatred, eyes half closed, red-faced with pleasure. Then suddenly, she gives her a stunning blow across the face.*

MARIE JEANNE. Strumpet! Priest's trollop! A mattress ready for any man to lie on and she can't even say no! He's a priest, is my son, do you hear? He's not for your great red hands, you skivvy! Take your shoes off and wash your floor!

ADELE [*shouting in her face*]. He's not a priest yet! He told me so! He can still say no!

MARIE JEANNE. Just let me catch him saying no, that's all! What—for a girl like you? [*She turns her around roughly.*] Wash your floor, slattern! My son, if you please! That I sweated blood to turn into a decent churchman! A little gentleman almost! [ADELE *has sunk down at the table, sobbing, her head on her arms.* MARIE JEANNE *goes over to her stove.*] Here. I'll make you your posset. You're so pitiful I'm sorry for you.

ADELE [*sobbing*]. I don't want it! It's too nasty.

MARIE JEANNE. It'll be nastier than yesterday's, and tomorrow's nastier than today's. I increase the dose each time. There are too many of us poor devils on this earth as it is. One less, that's always something.

ADELE [*sniffing*]. Have you told him?

MARIE JEANNE. Told who? I haven't told anybody. I don't fancy doing six months for your sweet sake, thank you!

ADELE. Him.

MARIE JEANNE [*with a great snort of mirth*]. Tell a priest? He'd have read me a sermon and offered to do the christening.

ADELE [*moaning*]. If he ever found out I'd kill myself!

MARIE JEANNE [*attentively stirring her brew over the stove*]. There's no rush. That'll come of its own when you're old and well worn out. Before that though, you'll have to sweat out all your tears, take all the blows you've got coming to you, wear out the hands the good God gave you scrubbing other people's kitchens—lie back on your hard bed night after night, without pleasure, with the first man who wants it lying on your belly. You haven't had your sackful yet, my girl. [*She comes back to her, almost tenderly.*] Here, you little fool, drink it down. I'll make you some good strong coffee after, to take the taste away. Proper coffee, some of mine, the genuine brew. [*She comes and sits down opposite her, elbows on the table.*] So you still won't tell me the fellow's name that did it to you?

ADELE [*stubbornly*]. No.

MARIE JEANNE. It's not Marcel, you're quite sure? He's always in your skirts these days.

ADELLE [*evasively*]. No, that's something else. He's got a job for me.

MARIE JEANNE [*softly, coaxing her to talk*]. A good job is it? Whereabouts?

ADELE. In a bar. In Algiers.

MARIE JEANNE [*between her teeth*]. Little bastard! I'll settle him, too. You never went with him, you're quite sure? Sometimes, it's hard to remember?

ADELE [*wearily*]. No, I tell you.

MARIE JEANNE. And that great gingerhaired milkman, you're sure it wasn't him?

ADELE. No, I tell you. [*Weeping like a child.*] Oh, it's too bitter. And I shall have pains again tonight. I'd rather throw myself in the river now and him with me, it'll be quicker.

MARIE JEANNE [*softly*]. Come on now girl, grit your teeth. It's bitter but it'll rid you of it. Another two bowls full and you never fell—you're virtuous. It's a lovely thing, is virtue. All you need is a flat belly. [*She asks abruptly.*] It wasn't Baron Jules, I trust?

ADELE. No.

MARIE JEANNE. Who was it then?

LEON *comes in from the stables, and shouts:*

LEON. Morning.

MARIE JEANNE. Morning. Wash your hands. And don't bother us. [*Turning back to* ADELE.] You're sure it wasn't that little jackadandy? You can lie with whomever you like, do you hear? But don't ever let one of the masters make love to you or you'll have some black blood in your heart that you won't ever spit out.

LEON [*impatiently, seated at the other end of the table*]. Where's my coffee then?

MARIE JEANNE. Shut your mouth, it's not made yet! [*She pushes the pot of brew over to him.*] Here. Have some of this. It's for thinning the belly down. It'll do you good, you bag of lard!

LEON [*pushing the pot away with a grimace*]. God, it stinks.

MARIE JEANNE. Not as much as you do. You've been stuffing down your bread and garlic again, you pig. And your jugful of red down the same hole, eh? And then we ask for our coffee, with our little finger cocked, all fancy airs! Coffee, is it? Why not finger bowls as well? And that's what I've been sleeping with these twenty years! [*She goes off with a throaty chuckle into the back kitchen.*]

LEON [*chortling as he shouts*]. Don't spit on the golden eggs! You've been coming back for more these twenty years and all!

MARIE JEANNE [*grinding her coffee upstage*]. Huh! One can't afford to be choosy, as my Grandma said when they made her coffin too short.

*The* AUTHOR, *who has come on stage again during the scene, says in an aggrieved murmur to the* SUPERINTENDENT:

AUTHOR. That's just inane.

SUPERINTENDENT [*indulgently*]. It's the sort of thing she'd say.

AUTHOR. Yes, but they'll think I wrote it in! That's the type of joke that lost me my good name in Paris. Abroad it doesn't matter so much, they can never translate them anyway.

SUPERINTENDENT [*watching* LEON's *tactics*]. I say, look at that, will you? The dirty great swine!

*Left alone,* ADELE *has turned her terrified gaze on* LEON. *She looks like a small animal caught in a trap. The man darts a look toward the scullery where* MARIE JEANNE *is busy grinding her coffee, oblivious of him. He gets up heavily, grabs the struggling* ADELE *and kisses her greedily.*

ADELE [*under her breath as she struggles*]. No! No! I don't want to! Not any more! [*She breaks free and runs up the stairs into the street.*]

AUTHOR [*worried*]. Now that's too unsavory, it really is. I would have wrapped it up a little, made it acceptable somehow. At least I wouldn't have shown the actual—— But now they've started making up their own lines, they're doing just as they please!

SUPERINTENDENT. Put your foot down. Interfere.

AUTHOR [*seeing* MARCEL *enter*]. Ssh . . .

MARCEL *has come into the kitchen. He goes over to the coachman who has gone back to his seat at the table. The* AUTHOR *watches intently.*

MARCEL [*sitting down*]. So?

LEON. So?

MARCEL. All right, then?

LEON. All right.

AUTHOR [*pained, from his corner*]. This dialogue!

*A pause.*

LEON [*after deep cogitation*]. All right, yourself?

MARCEL. All right. [*He has thought of something to say.*] You

know what the Sugarplum did? Rang for me twice again.
I'm dead.

*Enter* HUGUELINE.

HUGUELINE. Baron Jules has heaved himself out of bed. That
is, he's still in it, but he wants his breakfast.

MARIE JEANNE [*shouting from upstage*]. At this hour? It's not
ready!

HUGUELINE. Seems he has a trial gallop to go to. He's just got
to get there on time, then he'll know the winner of the
Grand Prix. Highly confidential. Only two in the secret,
him and the horse.

AUTHOR [*in his corner*]. Dull! Dull! It's all so dull! It's not
interesting, any of this stuff!

MARCEL [*perking up*]. That's very interesting indeed!

*At this, the* AUTHOR *feeling he has now lost all control, raises
his arms in impotent despair and wanders off with the* SUPER-
INTENDENT.

MARCEL. I don't think you quite realize what this means, my
pets. The winner of the Grand Prix. Touch wood, he'll be
an outsider like last year—he came in at forty-to-one. Come
on, Marie Jeanne, stir yourself. Make him his coffee, quick.
He just must be there on time. I've got five louis invested
in this.

MARIE JEANNE [*shouting from upstage*]. Five louis, you little
bastard, where did you steal that?

MARCEL [*preening himself*]. Night work!

*The little* SEMINARIST *appears suddenly at the top of the
inside staircase. He stops in surprise at seeing them all.* ADELE,
*who has appeared at the top of the area steps, looks at him
from a distance.*

SEMINARIST. Excuse me——

HUGUELINE [*calling up at him*]. Come in! Come in, your

reverence! We won't bite you. [*She shouts out to the back kitchen.*] Marie Jeanne, it's your little priest!

SEMINARIST. Excuse me, I only wanted——

MARIE JEANNE [*on the threshold of the back kitchen, says briefly*]. Go back upstairs.

SEMINARIST. But I wanted——

MARIE JEANNE. Upstairs! You don't belong down here. If you want something, ring for it. What do you think the bells are for? [*She shouts harshly.*] Do as I say! [*The* SEMINARIST *bows his head and goes upstairs.* MARIE JEANNE *goes to the table with the huge coffee pot, and sets it down among the bowls which* HUGUELINE *has distributed.*] There! Drink up, children!

HUGUELINE. What about Baron Jules? He's in a hurry.

MARIE JEANNE [*with a sort of grandeur*]. Hurry or no hurry, drink yours first. We've been working, we have. I'll pour some water on for him after.

*Swift blackout. The lights come on again suddenly. It seems as if the scene were beginning all over again.* MARIE JEANNE *and* ADELE *are alone in the kitchen.* MARIE JEANNE *is making her drink the brew.*

MARIE JEANNE. Drink, my fat lamb. Drink it down, my chick. He's starting to give up. He's loosening his little claws now. Losing his grip on life.

ADELE. It's so slow, it hurts so much.

MARIE JEANNE [*gently stroking her hair*]. Everything hurts. Everything is slow. Drink, my dove. Drink, my chick. We'll celebrate afterward, the two of us. We'll buy ourselves some goodies.

ADELE [*quietly*]. I'm not sorry about this one. But I'd like to have another, one day, with the boy I'll love.

MARIE JEANNE [*sitting down, suddenly dispirited*]. Ah, what fools we all are! Go to endless trouble. Risk six months in

jail for the darlings—for nothing, for friendship's sake;
they're already choosing a name for their next! [*She strokes
her hair gently.*] So you still won't tell who did this to you?

ADELE [*stonily*]. No. I can't.

MARIE JEANNE [*insidiously*]. Why can't you, my kitten? Why
won't you trust old Marie Jeanne? She's a wise old hen and
you know she always sets everything to rights. [*The SEMI-
NARIST appears suddenly at the top of the stairs, as he did
before. He stops, silent and pale. She shouts up at him.*]
Oh, so you're back, are you? What is it this time—shoe
polish? Coffee? Come to say Mass for us, have you? I told
you before, there are bells for the folk above stairs!

SEMINARIST [*very pale and articulating painfully*]. What are
you making her drink?

MARIE JEANNE [*harshly*]. Is that your business?

SEMINARIST. Yes. [*He comes downstairs with sudden courage,
snatches the bowl from the terrified girl and asks aggressively.*] What are you making her drink?

MARIE JEANNE [*chuckling, with an ugly glint in her eye*]. Taste
it. See for yourself. It's medicine for tummy ache. The girl
has tummy ache.

SEMINARIST [*puts the bowl down, shaking with rage and
shame*]. It's shameful!

MARIE JEANNE [*with a throaty laugh*]. Can't we have the belly
ache now, priest? Is it a sin suddenly?

SEMINARIST [*almost absurd, his voice broken by a sob*]. Don't
laugh! I forbid you to laugh about that!

MARIE JEANNE [*hard*]. I'm your mother. And I'll laugh when
I want, and about what I want, priest.

SEMINARIST [*dully*]. Yes, you're my mother. [*Hardening.*] I'll
leave the seminary. I'll marry her. I'll help her bring up the
child. Serving just one of God's poor and saving his soul is
as good as serving God.

MARIE JEANNE [*heavily, as she advances on him*]. Now you

listen to me, priest. Words don't impress me. You're a little
virgin with a dewdrop on the end of your nose. You still
think that words mean something, but you'll grow out of
that, like everybody else. You'll learn that life, real life, never
matches up with words. Meantime though, you're my son,
whether you fancy it or not. And I know what I want and
what I don't want. And I'm your mother.

SEMINARIST [*shouting with all his might*]. No!

MARIE JEANNE. Yes! [*She hits him twice across the face with
all her strength. She adds heavily.*] I'll throw her in the
river, in a sack, the slut, just as I'm going to throw her brat,
sooner than let you saddle yourself with her. Look at me,
take a good look. I don't give a rotten apple for laws and
policemen, or for the Lord above, either, not me, not Marie
Jeanne. Washing dishes in prison or doing the same thing
here until I drop down dead, it makes no odds to me. Look
at my hands. Look at them, look at your mother's hands.
[*She holds them out and says quickly.*] I swear to you I'll
strangle her with these two hands if I have to, but you'll
never marry a servant, never!

SEMINARIST. I'm a peasant and the son of a servant.

MARIE JEANNE [*dully*]. Yes, that's right. One's enough. You're
not having two in your life. I made you a priest to save you
from all that. [*A pause. She adds.*] Go back upstairs.

SEMINARIST. No.

MARIE JEANNE. You aren't old enough to say no to your
mother. [*She hits him again with all her might. He stands
his ground motionless and ashen pale.*] Upstairs!

*A pause. He glares at her, motionless. She holds his gaze, her
eyes blazing. A bell sounds in the kitchen. The bell board
lights up.*

SEMINARIST [*in a drained voice*]. They're ringing for you.

MARIE JEANNE. For the day's accounts. I know. To hell with

them. Go back up. You'll tell them that you've just had a letter calling you back to the seminary and that you have to take the evening train.

SEMINARIST. I'm a peasant, just like her. That child will live! I *will* marry her!

MARIE JEANNE. That child will die, by itself or along with her, but you'll not marry her, never! I can't stop you telling them back there that you don't want to be a priest. But I can stop you from marrying a slave. Now let me get on with my work.

SEMINARIST [*with a cry, touching and a little ridiculous*]. Nobody can fight the power of love!

MARIE JEANNE [*turning, fiery yet strangely calm*]. Yes, tom tit, I can. I've an old score to settle with love. And do you know how I settle my accounts? Look. [*She pulls a live rabbit out of a basket.*] It's easy. I'll show you. See?—*he* wants to live, he's one of God's creatures, too— But the master fancies a rabbit pasty tomorrow, so rabbits have to go through it. One second it takes me, a squeak, a wriggle, a smear of blood on his lips. [*She kills the rabbit under his nose.*] There. There's your love, whippet. [*She throws the dead rabbit in his face. He wipes his face, chalk white. Then he falls in a dead faint. She looks at him lying at her feet, then turns back to her work, grunting over her shoulder.*] Dishrag.

ADELE [*leaping up with a scream*]. You've killed him!

MARIE JEANNE [*wiping her hands*]. Don't be a fool. He's just fainted. Turnip juice in his veins. Thinks he can cut through mountains and can't even look life squarely in the face, for once.

ADELE *bends over the* SEMINARIST *and shakes him.*

ADELE. He's as white as a sheet. What should we do?

MARIE JEANNE [*unruffled*]. Give him a clout.

ADELE [*she murmurs*]. How white his skin is!

MARIE JEANNE *has come back to her and looks down at the boy.*

MARIE JEANNE [*softly*]. Yes, he's a fine gentleman. Except for his hands, those he gets from me. You should have seen him when he was a baby. I'd blush like a new bride when I bathed him. Not that I often had the chance. In those days we didn't even have the whole of Sunday afternoons off, and he was out in the country. Time to get there and back, that's all. [*She touches* ADELE's *hair gently as the girl strokes the little priest's head.*] You're a sensible girl, Adele. We're the same sort, you and I. Fine gentlemen aren't for us. I'm helping you. But you've got to help me, too, my lamb. You've got to tell him you don't want him. In two months he'll have got over it. And you'll be better off that way, too. One day he'd take it out of you for having married a servant girl. [ADELE *sobs with her head down on the boy's body. The old woman is crouched down beside her, still stroking her head, almost tenderly.*] Your heart's heavy now. I know. Mine was too, heavy to bursting. But you don't die of it—not of a bursting heart. [*She picks the bowl of brew off the table.*] Come on. Drink up your posset. So you'll have a flat belly if nothing else. [*She adds briskly.*] And then you can skin me my rabbit. With all these upsets I've killed him too soon. I shall have to cook him this morning.

*Sudden blackout.*

AUTHOR [*yelping in the darkness*]. For God's sake, not another blackout! If there's one thing I detest, it's that. It's too easy to black out here, there, and everywhere. [*The* SUPERINTENDENT *has lit a match. The* AUTHOR *strikes his cigarette lighter. We see their faces lit up in the surrounding dark. The*

AUTHOR *goes on, with rising ill-humor.*] I loathe this kind of drama. It's sheer blood and thunder. I don't care. I'm not putting my name to it!

SUPERINTENDENT [*sniffing a little*]. Damn good scene though, whatever you say. Just like a film.

AUTHOR. Your taste is deplorable, my dear man. The only thing I believe in is comedy.

SUPERINTENDENT. You should have written one then.

AUTHOR. Where has everybody gone? We'll have to get moving now, there's the whole play to be done yet. [*Shouting into the wings.*] Come along! On stage! On stage, everybody!

*Nobody comes. He storms out into the wings. The* SUPERINTENDENT *comes downstage and says confidentially to the audience:*

SUPERINTENDENT. I always said it would end in chaos. Doesn't it get on your nerves too, not knowing who killed the cook?

*Lights up. The* AUTHOR *comes back, downcast. The* SUPERINTENDENT *hails him jovially.*

SUPERINTENDENT. Well?

AUTHOR. They've vanished. Into thin air. That's what comes of not writing a play down.

SUPERINTENDENT. Lucky I'm still here, then.

AUTHOR [*sitting down gloomily*]. Yes. Not much though, is it?

SUPERINTENDENT. Suppose we finish the show on our own? I know a comic monologue by a Belgian writer, which is extremely funny.

AUTHOR. Oh, no, please! Look, just keep quiet, will you?

SUPERINTENDENT. Right. I won't say a word. But the mood's going to drop. Bound to. [*He makes a further suggestion.*] Perhaps you could recite the Nose speech from *Cyrano?*

*The* AUTHOR *annihilates him with a look. Enter the* SEMI-
NARIST.

SEMINARIST. My friends have appointed me to speak for them.
They're—how shall I put it?—ill at ease, hampered—yes,
that's it—hampered. . . . They feel that the pains you're
taking not to offend the audience—laudable though they are,
I'm sure—are preventing them from being themselves. This
is a grim story, sir, an inhuman story. But now it's begun,
now that it's half real—if we can't perform it honestly, then
we feel, my friends and I, that it would be best if we vanished into nothing again. Speaking for myself, never mind
what I may have to suffer, I must do what I have to do now.
You shouldn't have invented me and given me that pattern
of life and that mother, and sown the seeds of this shame
in me. . . . But you've done it. So now you must leave us
alone. And not interfere until the end. [*A pause. He says
quietly.*] If you're willing to leave it to us, I'll go upstairs and
do the children's scene and, after that, everything must take
its course. If not, then you must let us disappear.

*The* AUTHOR *listens, his head in his hands. He says simply,
without moving, no longer at all funny now:*

AUTHOR. Yes, do as you think best. As a matter of fact, I was
going to tell you . . . first of all that I shouldn't perhaps
have done it, and then . . . [*He says suddenly.*] I'm sorry,
my boy. You know, you think and think, you turn ideas over
in your mind and . . .

SEMINARIST [*quietly*]. The harm's done now. And who knows,
perhaps this is better than not being alive at all.

*He goes out. The lights go out below stairs. Above they come
up slowly. The two children are seen kneeling for their evening
prayers before the table which is littered with their school
books. The* SEMINARIST *has come in and goes to kneel beside
them. The* COUNTESS *enters quietly and listens to the prayers.*

*Down below, the* SUPERINTENDENT *has moved a little to one side. One can just make out the anguished* AUTHOR, *sitting alone in the gloom, watching and listening.*

CHILDREN [*together*]. Our Father, we beg You to keep all things good and pure as you created them. Keep our dear father and mother in health and . . . [*They stop.*] and peace of mind and spirit. We beg you also for . . .

SEMINARIST. Your special blessing. . . .

CHILDREN. Your special blessing on our little brother Thibaut who has just come into the world, so that he may receive in abundance . . .

SEMINARIST. All your most precious gifts . . .

CHILDREN. All your most precious gifts. Amen. [*They get up with a clatter.*]

ELDER BOY. Mamma, may we play for a little while before we go to bed? We've been very good today.

YOUNGER BOY [*echoing him*]. Very good today.

COUNTESS. Go up and play in your room for five minutes, and don't make a noise and don't wake your brother, and then ask Nurse to get you ready for bed.

ELDER BOY [*on his way out*]. Thank you, Mamma. Mamma, will you tell her that we've said our prayers? She never believes us and she makes us say them all over again. It's a dreadful bore.

YOUNGER BOY [*echoing him*]. Dreadful bore.

COUNTESS [*smiling*]. Yes, I'll tell her.

*They go out. The* SEMINARIST, *looking white and drawn, has gathered up his books. He stops.*

SEMINARIST. May I speak to you a moment, Madame? [*The* COUNTESS *stops on her way out and looks at him, rather surprised at his tone. The* SEMINARIST *goes on abruptly.*] Your Grace, I can't go on hearing the children say their prayers. I can't pray myself any more.

COUNTESS [*taken aback, murmurs*]. Father Thomas——

SEMINARIST. You're good and kind, I know you are. I daresay I'm very young—and impressionable, and inept as well, I expect . . . [*He adds.*] Perhaps I'm unworthy, too? I can't devote myself as I should to those two young souls. I am going to take the liberty of asking you to . . . [*His voice trails away. He looks quite lost.*]

COUNTESS [*gently*]. Calm yourself, Father Thomas. Yes, you do seem deeply troubled. . . . Personally, we're very happy indeed with you and your influence on the children.

SEMINARIST [*recovering a little*]. I suppose it's because I'm very young, and come from a modest background. . . . But there is something in the sight of this peace, this happiness, in the sight of those two good and charming children, miraculously shielded from all taint—all contact with the horrible reality of things . . . and all this so close—a few feet away from everything that's most sordid and hideous in life. . . . Something . . . [*He feels for words, anguished.*] some appalling mockery which could make me doubt my vocation.

COUNTESS. I don't quite understand you, Father Thomas.

SEMINARIST [*bewildered, as if to himself*]. If I'm to be a priest in spite of it, I shall ask to serve in the poorest, the most bereft of parishes, so I can mingle with them, set myself lower even than they. I want them to sit down to table, just once, while I wait on them. I want it to be me who scours their greasy pans afterward, in the stink and filth that sticks to the fingers. [*He cries out feverishly.*] And yet I hate all of that! I hate the poor! I hate poverty and dirt, it turns my stomach!

*He sinks down sobbing, with his head on the speechless* COUNTESS' *lap. She makes a tentative move to touch his hair and murmurs:*

COUNTESS. Yes, you are indeed very young. Calm yourself, Father Thomas. Or rather, cry a little. It will do you good. Then we'll have a little talk and I'll try to help you. That is, if only I can manage to understand you.

SEMINARIST [*lifting his head and looking at her, his eyes hard*]. You won't be able to. You're kind and yet you won't be able to. [*He says abruptly.*] Madame, downstairs, working in your kitchens, there is a girl, a very poor girl . . . I don't think you can conceive what the cruelty of men and of life can inflict on one single human creature—someone who, despite it all, has stayed innocent and pure. But you might be able to help. You should be able to find something deep in your heart. Something real, something else besides those improving words or those paltry sums that people use to shake off the poor. Oh, if you could only think of something that would, just once, draw a smile from the pitiless justice of God!

*He has dropped down again, sobbing, his head on her lap. The* COUNTESS, *near to tears herself, says gently, with the same shy, unfinished gesture toward his head:*

COUNTESS. You move me very deeply, Father Thomas. I promise I shall do my best, with your help, to think of something I might do for this girl. Tell me a little more about her. Who is she?

*The lights have gone down until one can barely distinguish the two characters. They both go out. The lights come up again on the* AUTHOR *and the* SUPERINTENDENT.

SUPERINTENDENT [*moist-eyed and sniffing as always after this kind of scene*]. So that's when she decided, I gather, to go below stairs and ask the girl to be godmother to her new baby?

AUTHOR [*dully, as if ashamed*]. Yes. It's frightful.

SUPERINTENDENT. Why? I think it's rather a sweet idea, myself.

AUTHOR [*quietly*]. No, my dear man. You really don't understand much, do you? It was horrible. [*The servants have come in down below in the gloom. They get into a line and seem to be waiting. The* AUTHOR *rises and pulls the* SUPERINTENDENT *away.*] Come along. Let's leave them. I can't watch this, it's too painful.

SUPERINTENDENT. Oh, but . . . ?

*The* AUTHOR *shrugs helplessly. They go out. Up above, the lights are dazzling bright now. The* COUNTESS *comes in quickly, followed by the* COUNT. *He is in evening dress and carries a top hat and cane. He was clearly about to go out.*

COUNT. You cannot do this, it's sheer folly!

COUNTESS. Forgive me, my dear, but I am going to do it.

COUNT [*fighting to keep calm*]. Evangeline, I have never ordered you to do anything and I ask your pardon beforehand for what may seem rather ridiculous in my new role as head of the family, but this concerns my son. I forbid you to do what you are planning.

COUNTESS [*quietly*]. I shall go down. And I shall do it. Forgive me for sounding a little high-flown, too, but God himself has commanded me to do this.

COUNT [*shrugging, says a little curtly*]. God has never commanded anyone to do anything grotesque. Evangeline, for the first time, you disappoint me. You are still quite young, I may not be as entertaining as I fondly imagine, and perhaps you are bored. That I can understand. But for you to plunge into religious mania merely because you don't know what to do with yourself—that I will not tolerate. Take a lover—dammit!—a suitable lover. I'd find it less shaming.

COUNTESS [*smiling gently*]. But I should be ashamed, my dear. I'm much less broadminded than you are. I know that your pride and your vanity—forgive the word—are very easily hurt. But don't disappoint me yourself, for the first time. Let me go down and do what I have planned to do.

COUNT [*icily*]. It's impossible.

COUNTESS. Why? I want to give that young girl this great gift. I want, for once—for things to be different from the way they've always been before.

COUNT. Evangeline, you're not only naïve, you're being ridiculous now. Your Aunt de Guermantes was to have been godmother to the child.

COUNTESS. My Aunt de Guermantes is a great lady. She'll understand that there was somebody above her in the eyes of God who would honor Thibaut more than she. The poorest girl in the house. [*More gravely.*] I am a religious person, Thibaut, and this is the first time—that I've felt I was about to do something which approaches, just a little, what Christ demanded of us. Something other than an empty gesture.

COUNT [*shouting with irritation*]. That's exactly what it will be—a gesture! And a theatrical one, which is worse. A mere sop to your vanity.

COUNTESS [*genuinely astonished*]. My vanity? I'm going to ask a servant to be godmother to my son and that's vanity?

COUNT. Of the worst kind. The poor have no use for your words and your good intentions. They've no use for your great tender loving soul. They've no use for your vanity. They have only one craving, one demand, and that is to be respected, like the rest of us. You can only honor with your masquerade a dyed-in-the-wool domestic like Romain. If that girl has any quality at all you'll hurt her feelings, that's all.

COUNTESS. How can you possibly know? You're an unfeeling, frivolous man. You've no heart.

COUNT [*curtly*]. I have the heart I was born with, my dear.

I told you that I once made the experiment which you are proposing to try. And it was a failure.

COUNTESS [*with almost malicious irony, suddenly*]. My dear, I fear we may lapse into the worst vulgarity if we argue on that subject. It isn't because you had an affair with one of your first wife's chambermaids twenty years ago that makes you sole judge of the way those poor people may think—people who are much better and more honest than you are, I assure you.

COUNT. They are neither better nor more honest. They are profoundly different, that's all. And they know it. That's why they require us to behave properly. I loved Marie Jeanne.

COUNTESS [*turning away*]. We won't talk about that, if you don't mind. It's odious.

COUNT [*hard*]. It is odious, but we will talk about it. I loved Marie Jeanne. The Countess was only the wife my father chose for me. Marie Jeanne was my real wife, for five whole years. I shall spare you the details.

COUNTESS [*tersely*]. It might be as well.

COUNT. With as acute an awareness, believe me, as I have today of the folly I was preparing to commit, I made plans to go away with her, hide away somewhere, and be happy. My fortune was then entirely in my wife's hands, just as my present fortune is entirely in yours. I have never possessed anything but my name and a great many neckties. And I am probably unemployable. But I used to paint. . . . Yes. You never knew that, and I haven't painted since, but, yes, I used to paint. And Lautrec, who's a vague cousin of mine, used to assure me that I had talent. I told that—I told that young person—yes, that's the word—that I could earn our living, not by selling my pictures, I wasn't as conceited as that—but perhaps by giving art lessons somewhere abroad. So, that young person, who had nothing to lose and who loved me—you can believe that if I tell you so today—that young person said no. *She* said it. It was she who said I shouldn't do this and why. It was she who told me—with pride—that we came from different worlds and that love was merely a commonplace accident. And from that day, she broke with me completely. And so that it would be really final, really definite, she gave herself to a stable boy who was courting her. She must still be his mistress, she was a girl who didn't care for change. He became our coachman, if you want the whole story. And since then, she's stayed below stairs and I was never able to see her again.

COUNTESS [*dully, after a pause*]. And you went on living on the upper floors and left her below stairs. [*A pause.*] You sicken me.

COUNT [*rigidly*]. I went on living, as you say. As well as possible, too, for I consider that a duty. And, I might add, my duty toward her, who had wanted it so in the artless pride of her sacrifice.

COUNTESS [*in a murmur*]. How loathsome.

COUNT [*coldly*]. Yes. How loathsome. But that's how it was. This girl, who taught me that there were—forgive a very pompous phrase, I'm aware of being slightly grotesque at the moment—that there were human beings—— [*He searches for the right word.*] great enough—they are rare, but there are some—to look reality in the face. [*He breaks off, lights a cigar, and sits down, his old ironical, inconsequent self again.*] Now I've warned you what to expect. I can't restrain you bodily, or lock you in your room.

*The* SEMINARIST *knocks discreetly on the door. He comes in shyly, his eyes shining.*

SEMINARIST. Your Grace, they're waiting for us.

COUNTESS [*abruptly*]. Let us go down.

*She goes out with him. The lights have come up again down below, where the servants are still waiting.*

ROMAIN. Come along now—in your ranks—in your ranks. Marcel, Hugueline, Adele, Alexis—stand in line. A little patience, good people. Her Ladyship won't be long now. [*A pause. He turns stiffly to* MARIE JEANNE.] Madame Marie Jeanne, I have been in the profession long enough to learn that the exclusive tribe of lady cooks is particularly jealous of its little privileges. Nevertheless, for the last time, will you be so obliging as to put on your cap?

MARIE JEANNE. No.

ROMAIN. But you wear it when you go up with your accounts in the morning!

MARIE JEANNE. I do as I please. I've never worn a cap in my own kitchen.

ROMAIN [*with sinister dignity*]. Then there will be a lapse.

*Just then, on the main staircase, one sees the* COUNTESS, *the* NURSE *carrying the baby, the* SEMINARIST *and the* CHILDREN, *all descending in procession to the kitchens.* ADELE, *who has been making a brave effort to remain on her feet, suddenly falls fainting into the others' arms.*

ADELE. I don't think I can stand much longer.

ROMAIN [*rushing over, yelping*]. Now what? A fine thing! And just as her Grace is coming down! Get up! On your feet, girl! Stand up straight.

*He gives her a violent slap to bring her to her senses. There is complete confusion down below. Everyone crowds round the unconscious* ADELE. *Old* ROMAIN *runs to and fro squealing, in a frantic attempt to control his staff.*

In your ranks! In your ranks, this instant!

*At this second the* COUNTESS *comes in with her two boys, followed by the* NURSE *in beribboned cap and apron, cere-*

*moniously carrying the new baby in his froth of lace, followed
by the* SEMINARIST, *who is near to tears with emotion. The*
COUNTESS *stops in astonishment.*

COUNTESS. Why, what's the matter? Is that young girl ill?

ROMAIN. A slight mishap, your Ladyship. It's nothing. Nothing at all. The excitement. There, you see, she's coming
round. Get up, you! On your feet! Stand in line!

*The* COUNTESS, *amid the general curiosity, moves to the dazed*
ADELE, *who has been led back to her place and is being held
up by her fellow servants. The* COUNTESS *stops in front of her.*

COUNTESS [*graciously*]. Mademoiselle, it is you I have come
to see. And I wanted all your friends to be there, too, around
you. Look at this little boy, my dear. He is my youngest
child. His name is Thibaut, like his papa. But that's the
name his Grace and I chose for him when he was born. He
is to have another, which is the name he will be christened
with, and that second name I shall ask you to choose.
[ADELE *looks at her, dazed. The* COUNTESS *goes on.*] Mademoiselle, I have come down to ask if you would be so kind
as to be godmother to my son. [*There is a stunned silence
in the kitchen.* ADELE *stares at her in mute incomprehen-
sion. The* COUNTESS *smiles.*] I know you're surprised. But
this can only astonish those who do not know that courage
and a humble heart are the greatest virtues we should honor.
I am sure you will help me to teach them to our little
Thibaut and that, later on, he will be proud to have a godmother like you. [ADELE *continues to stare at her, dazed.
The* COUNTESS *goes blithely on, to the increasing embarrassment of all present save* ROMAIN, *who is clucking like an
enraptured turkey.*] Come. You must get to know each other.
You must take him in your arms. [*She takes the baby from
the* NURSE *and puts it in* ADELE'S *arms. The girl looks at it,
stunned and speechless. Then suddenly, she lets out a wild*

*animal howl, puts the baby in the* COUNTESS' *arms, and runs out into the back kitchen. The* COUNTESS *stands there, in dumb bewilderment.*]

ROMAIN [*screeching*]. It's outrageous! Outrageous! Such an honor! Fetch her back, you others! Fetch her back this instant!

*Some of the servants have run out after* ADELE, *who is at the scullery table, sobbing. They call out:*

VOICES. She won't come! She says she won't come!

ROMAIN [*near to hysteria, the blazing justicer*]. Carry her then —bring her back! Bound hand and foot! Halter round her neck!

*He tears out like a madman, perhaps to hang himself. The others have succeeded in bringing back* ADELE. *They drag her over to the* COUNTESS. ADELE *screams and struggles like one possessed.*

ADELE. No! I don't want to see it! I don't want to see her child! [*They hold her in front of the* COUNTESS. *She screams out at her suddenly, like a madwoman.*] I've a baby in my belly that I'm trying to get rid of! That's why I fainted!

COUNTESS [*stammering*]. A baby?—what baby?

ADELE [*yelling, suddenly vulgar, her hair disheveled*]. A child that isn't born yet, just like yours, only mine's the coachman's! The coachman who raped me one night in the stables when I went to take him a bucket. In the dung! I came back with my dress covered in dung and the others laughed at me, because they thought I'd fallen down and that's why I was crying. [*She shouts at* LEON, *who has retreated behind the others.*] Don't run away! You're braver, aren't you, when you're alone with me? Behind the doors, against the wall, every time he can get me in a corner he takes me. And I can't even scream because I'm afraid the others will know, and I'm too ashamed, on account of his wife. And he stinks! And he hurts me and I don't like him! [*She glares at them all suddenly, with queenly grandeur.*] I don't like anybody! Not even her, who pretends she's good and kind and makes me medicines so that I'll drop it, in between boxing my ears. Those that hit me I don't like. Not even him, with his God, who said he loved me and didn't have the guts to tear me out of his mother's claws and who couldn't think of anything better than to go sniveling upstairs so you would bring me your brat. Those that haven't any guts—I don't like them, either. [*She looks at them all like a small cornered animal.*] I hate you all! My mother sent me into service when I was twelve years old. I'll never forgive you for it, any of you! And my first master, he used to try it on too, even then, and so his mistress beat me, but she kept me on just the same because all I got was my food and there was nobody else at that price that she could knock about and work to death—from five in the morning—yes, Milady, five!—right until eleven o'clock at night! And no Sundays off, either! [*She screams at them, her eyes blazing.*] That's another thing I shan't forgive any of you for, ever! [*She looks at them all as they stand there, dumb and frozen. She glares at the* SEMINARIST, *her kindly little face distorted with hatred.*] And before that, priest boy, I was with the nuns! And that was worse, because I was the smallest. When you'd said a bad word in the sewing room, they'd put you out in the yard in winter, with your bum in icy water, and you'd have to sit there while the others filed past you, laughing, with your arse in the wet. [*She yells at the* COUNTESS, *ashen, as if the word was an exorcism.*] Arse in the wet, Milady! Arse! Arse! Arse! Do you hear? And you had to tell God you were sorry as well! [*She shouts, her eyes blazing.*] I don't like God!

MARIE JEANNE *goes to her and says heavily:*

MARIE JEANNE. That's enough now.

ADELE [*with a shiver, goes on more quietly*]. After that, I went to work for the chemist. He left me alone, that one. But his wife thought I was too good-looking. So she made up some tale or other. . . . I was fifteen.

*And suddenly she sinks gently down on the ground like a bleeding rag in the midst of the appalled onlookers. There is a moment of stupor, nobody dares to move, then suddenly the* AUTHOR *tears in from the wings, bellowing:*

AUTHOR. Stop! Stop! Stop! It's impossible! [*Going to the* COUNTESS.] Go back upstairs, Madame, go up, you're going to faint as well in a minute. I always knew this would happen. I always said we mustn't do this scene. It was an open door for the worst vulgarity, for sheer filth. [*He takes the baby and gives it to the* NURSE.] You, take that! And follow your mistress. Go back upstairs, Madame. And try to forget this painful scene. You meant well. Go back upstairs. Upstairs. This whole thing is lamentable and it's entirely my fault. I should never have started it. [*He pushes the* COUNTESS *out. He watches as the others lead* ADELE *out.*] Poor little soul, we mustn't blame her too much. She should never have been submitted to this ordeal. It's useless cruelty. [*He cries out ridiculously.*] Useless! I can't believe that life is as ugly as that. Good Lord, there are decent people everywhere! It's our duty to say so and to write plays with good kind people in them and good wholesome sentiments. And to the devil with literature.

*He goes out. Only three people are left on the stage:* LEON, MARIE JEANNE, *and the* SEMINARIST. *The* SUPERINTENDENT *eyes them keenly from behind a flat.*

MARIE JEANNE [*softly*]. You scum.

LEON [*harshly*]. That's enough of that. You've done worse. And before I ever did.

MARIE JEANNE. Not at the same time as you. And I told you about it. I played fair.

LEON [*cackling*]. I know! The leftovers! For the servants' hall. As usual.

MARIE JEANNE [*shouting at him*]. Even the leftovers were too good for you! Did you ever look at yourself beside him?

LEON. I've never been beside him. In the carriage, I've got my backside to him and he's never set foot in the stables.

MARIE JEANNE. Doing a thing like that—to *me!* With that dishrag. Under my very eyes. [*She cries with magnificent outrage.*] Under my own roof!

LEON [*nose to nose with her*]. You're a servant here, just like the rest of us. It's not your own roof. [*They stare at each other silently. He goes on, thickly.*] If you want to know, she's not the first. That other one whose brat you got rid of, too. He was one of mine as well. It was for me you risked going to jail.

MARIE JEANNE [*in her teeth*]. You bastard. [*She seizes a knife from the table.*]

SEMINARIST. No!

LEON [*drawing his own knife*]. Easy. No games. You stick me, I'll stick you. I'm warning you—this is man to man.

MARIE JEANNE [*with a terrible smile*]. Do you think any man can scare me?

SEMINARIST [*yelling suddenly*]. Stop it!

MARIE JEANNE *turns to him, as if hitherto unaware of his presence.*

MARIE JEANNE. Go back upstairs. You're the other one's son, the one upstairs. I got you from him in a dark corner, too. Go and join him. You're a mongrel. [*She and* LEON *have begun to circle around each other like two jungle beasts.*]

SEMINARIST [*shouting*]. You can't! You've no right to! You're
my mother! [*He hurls himself onto* MARIE JEANNE *in an
attempt to disarm her.*] You're my mother!

*Sudden blackout. The* SUPERINTENDENT *who has been following the fight, can be heard in the dark, shouting in great excitement.*

SUPERINTENDENT. Lights! Turn on the lights, curse you! Just
when we were going to find out!

*The curtain has come down in the blackout. The lights go up
again on the front cloth. Across it come* BARON JULES *and the*
BARONESS, *in full evening dress.*

BARON. I tell you it *is* this way!

BARONESS. We'll get lost!

BARON. We'll make ourselves late, which is more to the point.
And you're going to twist your ankle.

BARONESS. It's a humane duty, my dear. Besides, it won't take
five minutes.

BARON. Oh, very well.

*The* BARON *and* BARONESS *go through the curtain, which rises
as soon as they are in position behind it.*

*All the servants except* LEON *and* ROMAIN *are gathered round*
MARIE JEANNE, *who is lying on the kitchen table. The* SUPER-
INTENDENT *and the* SEMINARIST *have gone.*

BARONESS. What's this, Marie Jeanne, my dear? I hear you
aren't too well.

MARIE JEANNE [*grunting*]. So the rumor runs. I feel fine.

BARON. It's too absurd, the whole thing. One should never
play with firearms. Accidents happen so easily. It was a
quarrel, wasn't it?

MARIE JEANNE. Yes, a little tiff. Not even that. It's very good
of you to bother, and your Ladyship too. It will soon be
over.

BARON [*finding the idea most convenient*]. Yes, it will, won't it? A few days in bed and it won't even show.

MARIE JEANNE [*gently roguish*]. And I expect you're late, as usual.

BARON [*laughing*]. You old witch, Marie Jeanne! She always guesses everything. Marie Jeanne, you look splendid. [*To his wife.*] My dear, it's ten minutes to twelve. If we don't want to miss the President——

BARONESS. Yes, Marie Jeanne, dear, we're going to a ball at the opera, do you see, with the President and the Republican Guard and everything. The whole gaudy flummery. Don't think it's fun for us, it isn't. We'd just as soon stay here with you. Positively. They're always so fatuous, those gala occasions. But the diplomatic corps is on duty, you see, and we promised Coco we'd be there, so she wouldn't die of boredom. Coco is the Austrian Ambassadress.

MARIE JEANNE [*smiling between two spasms of pain*]. Oh, yes, I was thinking to myself, I've heard that name before! She's the one who likes my mushroom tart.

BARONESS [*delighted with this little touch*]. Yes! That's Coco! But when we heard you'd been hurt, we simply had to come down, Ambassadress or no Ambassadress. She'll wait for us.

BARON [*looking again at his watch*]. Well, for a bit, anyway.

BARONESS. For as long as necessary. We're very fond of you, you know, Marie Jeanne. We positively are.

BARON [*fidgeting*]. We'll draw attention to ourselves when we go into the Embassy box, my dear.

BARONESS. Oh, don't complain, there's nothing you like more.

BARON [*anxious to make an end of it*]. Take care, my old dear. Get well soon, so you can make us those splendid little dishes of yours again. We think a lot of you, you know, in this house!

MARIE JEANNE [*with a smile*]. I should think you do.

BARONESS. Until tomorrow. We'll come down again. Take good care of yourself. [*She blows a kiss with her gloved fingertips.*] Be brave! We'll be thinking of you.

BARON [*on his way out*]. When I got kicked that time in the paddock at Longchamps, I thought I was dead. And you see?—not a bit of it. It's bad while it lasts, that's all.

MARIE JEANNE. It won't. Careful of those steps, your Lordship. They're slippery.

BARON [*blithely*]. I'm used to them. Positively.

BARONESS [*babyishly as she steps out*]. 'Bye! 'Bye! 'Bye!

*They go up the stairs in a flurry of satin and scent.*

MARIE JEANNE [*to* HUGUELINE]. Did you tell him, up there, to come down?

HUGUELINE. Yes.

MARIE JEANNE. Then leave me, all of you. I'll wait for him. [*To* ALEXIS.] I was a queen once, boy, when I was twenty. The loveliest thighs in Nice. I'm cold. Put my big red cloak over me. [ALEXIS *goes to the cupboard and brings back* MARIE JEANNE's *big red woollen cloak. He is holding the crown in his hand.*] Put my crown here, beside me.

ADELE, *who has been standing a little apart from the others, dressed in a shabby little coat, goes to pick up a cheap suitcase which she has deposited in a corner. She nods to* MARCEL.

ADELE. Take me to that little lodging house you told me about. And then, in five or six days, when I'm better, you can write to that friend of yours and say I'm taking the boat. [*She picks up the case.* MARCEL *takes it from her kindly.*]

MARCEL. Here, give it to me. It's the least I can do. You know, my pet, if you set about it right, you can make your niche out there. And keep your head above water. There aren't so many ways of doing that. You're in pain. Here, lean on me. . . .

*They go up the area steps and out into the street.* MARIE
JEANNE *has not moved. The others have disappeared. The
kitchen seems darker. It becomes an earthly place, full of
strange, fantastic shadows. Only the portrait of the Old Lady
up above is still faintly lit, and likewise* MARIE JEANNE,
*stretched out on the table covered with her red cloak, her
crown beside her, like an aged queen. Now she begins to talk
to herself, as if in delirium. Young* ALEXIS *will come in later
and start to peel his vegetables. During her monologue, the*
AUTHOR *comes in quietly and sits on a stool beside her, without her seeing him at first.*

MARIE JEANNE [*softly*]. The loveliest thighs in Nice. They told
me so when they gave me the prize. And on one single
Sunday, more flowers than the Old Girl got in twenty years
in return for her dinner parties! [*She smiles a mysterious
smile.*] Talk about a scandal! Her Ladyship's maid taking
the liberty of putting herself forward! She nearly threw me
out, only you got angry. That's the first time I ever saw you
angry. You who always made a joke of everything. You
looked so handsome in your anger. So then she went into
her room and slammed the door and for five years you didn't
speak to each other. [*She smiles with happiness.*] For me.
[*She murmurs tenderly.*] Thank you, my darling, for letting
me be queen for one whole Sunday. [*She suddenly feels the
presence of somebody beside her.*] Your Grace, is that you,
my love?

AUTHOR [*gently*]. No. He's still busy upstairs. The Countess
has had a nervous attack. They're waiting for the doctor.

MARIE JEANNE [*smiling*]. I knew he wouldn't come down.
That's the way we've lived, there's no reason why it
shouldn't be like that when we die—each of us on his own
floor. [*She asks, suddenly suspicious.*] Look here, you, what
possessed you to start telling people about me?

AUTHOR [*disconcerted*]. Why, Marie Jeanne, dear——

MARIE JEANNE. Don't you dear me! In the first place, he didn't
call me Marie Jeanne. It was you who invented that. He
used to call me "little fellow" and, in bed, some other name
that I don't want to say. But what gave you the idea of
talking about me? You never knew me.

AUTHOR [*gently*]. Yes, I did. Very well.

MARIE JEANNE [*ingenuously*]. Did we meet somewhere? [*She
giggles.*] Socially?

AUTHOR. No. Not socially.

MARIE JEANNE [*chuckling*]. Oh, I see. I was going to say . . . !
[*A pause; she asks suspiciously.*] Did you know him—his
Grace, I mean?

AUTHOR. Yes, slightly.

MARIE JEANNE. He was handsome. When we went upstairs to
peep through the door at the revels, he was always the
handsomest of all the gentlemen.

AUTHOR [*bashfully*]. Oh, come . . .

MARIE JEANNE [*furiously*]. He was, I tell you! Do you think
I'd have kept my heart for him, as well as everything else
of me, if he hadn't been the handsomest? You don't know
women! Five years I stayed faithful to you. For five years
I didn't go dancing with the others, not one single Sunday.
Five years. That's a lifetime for a girl with fire in her belly.
[*She murmurs suddenly, amused.*] It's a funny thing, love.
There's no telling where it'll go and hide itself.

AUTHOR [*quietly*]. Yes, it's a funny thing.

*She feels the presence of someone.*

MARIE JEANNE. Who's there?

ALEXIS. Me, Alexis.

MARIE JEANNE. What are you doing?

ALEXIS. Peeling my potatoes. With all this to-do I haven't
finished my pile yet.

MARIE JEANNE [*softly*]. Peel away, lad, peel away. The soup comes before everything. [A *pause.*] What are you going to do when you grow up?

ALEXIS. I shall run a restaurant.

MARIE JEANNE. Will you be the boss?

ALEXIS. Yes. I've started saving up already. I never spend anything. I'm thirteen now. So, in ten or fifteen years, down in Nice . . .

MARIE JEANNE [*a smile lighting up her face*]. Oh, in Nice? It's lovely, Nice. [*She asks.*] Down in Nice, what?

ALEXIS. My restaurant. On the old port.

MARIE JEANNE. And you think you'll forget all the beatings?

ALEXIS. Pooh. You have to learn your trade. Then after you're grown up, you forget, when you're a man. I'll be a man. And a man's strong, a man's free, he does what he likes. He can be a king, a man can, if he wants.

MARIE JEANNE [*incredulously*]. What—despite the rich?

ALEXIS [*clear-eyed*]. But I'll be rich.

*He goes on calmly peeling his potatoes. The clock can be heard ticking away. Up on the main staircase one sees the* COUNT, *in evening dress and cloak, returning from his club, a lonely figure.*

MARIE JEANNE [*murmuring*]. Your Grace?

AUTHOR. Yes, little fellow, I'm here.

MARIE JEANNE. Am I beautiful, your Grace?

*The* AUTHOR *looks at the old woman dying in her tattered finery. He murmurs tenderly:*

AUTHOR. Yes, you're beautiful. [*He draws closer to her, takes her hand, and kisses it.*]

MARIE JEANNE [*in ecstasy*]. My hand . . . just like a lady! [*A bell rings. Automatically, she sits up, like the little servant girl in her attic room years ago, and murmurs.*] They're ringing for me.

*The* AUTHOR *goes to her quietly and makes her lie down again.*

AUTHOR. Rest. I'll go up and see.

*He draws aside a little. The kitchen boy goes on peeling. The clock ticks. Suddenly the ticking stops. The* AUTHOR *goes to the kitchen boy and ushers him out. Then he comes back to* MARIE JEANNE, *and with a gesture almost like a caress, he closes her eyes. He lights a rare cigarette beside the make-believe corpse. The* SUPERINTENDENT *comes in abruptly.*

SUPERINTENDENT. Well?

AUTHOR [*giving him a cold stare*]. Well, what?

SUPERINTENDENT. I've found out who killed the old woman.

AUTHOR [*his thoughts elsewhere*]. Oh yes? Who was it?

SUPERINTENDENT. The coachman. Thirty-five minutes' interrogation with two of my lads, American style, with lights in his eyes, and he confessed. The case is all sewn up. Basically, you see, this story of yours was quite simple. It was you who were inclined to complicate it.

AUTHOR. You think so? Well, you can disappear now. You can go back to your nothingness. It's over.

*The* SUPERINTENDENT *goes out riled. The* AUTHOR *turns to the audience.*

Excuse the author for his shortcomings, ladies and gentlemen. But this is a play he never could manage to write.

*It is hoped that despite it all he does get some applause, and he goes out.*

*The Curtain Falls.*

# DRAMABOOKS

PLAYS

MD 1 *Christopher Marlowe* (Tamburlaine the Great, Parts I & II, Doctor Faustus, The Jew of Malta, Edward the Second)
MD 2 *William Congreve* (Complete Plays)
MD 3 *Webster and Tourneur* (The White Devil, The Duchess of Malfi, The Atheist's Tragedy, The Revenger's Tragedy)
MD 4 *John Ford* (The Lover's Melancholy, 'Tis Pity She's a Whore, The Broken Heart, Love's Sacrifice, Perkin Warbeck)
MD 5 *Richard Brinsley Sheridan* (The Rivals, St. Patrick's Day, The Duenna, A Trip to Scarborough, The School for Scandal, The Critic)
MD 6 *Camille and Other Plays* (Scribe: A Peculiar Position, and The Glass of Water; Sardou: A Scrap of Paper; Dumas, *fils*: Camille; Augier: Olympe's Marriage)
MD 7 *John Dryden* (The Conquest of Granada, Parts I & II, Marriage à la Mode, Aureng-Zebe)
MD 8 *Ben Jonson* Vol. 1 (Volpone, Epicoene, The Alchemist)
MD 9 *Oliver Goldsmith* (The Good Natur'd Man, She Stoops to Conquer, An Essay on the Theatre, A Register of Scotch Marriages)
MD 10 *Jean Anouilh* Vol. 1 (Antigone, Eurydice, The Rehearsal, Romeo and Jeannette, The Ermine)
MD 11 *Let's Get a Divorce! and Other Plays* (Labiche: A Trip Abroad, and Célimare; Sardou: Let's Get a Divorce!; Courteline: These Cornfields; Feydeau: Keep an Eye on Amélie; Prévert: A United Family; Achard: Essay on Feydeau)
MD 12 *Jean Giraudoux* Vol. 1 (Ondine, The Enchanted, The Madwoman of Chaillot, The Apollo of Bellac)
MD 13 *Jean Anouilh* Vol. 2 (Restless Heart, Time Remembered, Ardèle, Mademoiselle Colombe, The Lark)
MD 14 *Henrik Ibsen: The Last Plays* (Little Eyolf, John Gabriel Borkman, When We Dead Awaken)
MD 15 *Ivan Turgenev* (A Month in the Country, A Provincial Lady, A Poor Gentleman)
MD 16 *George Farquhar* (The Constant Couple, The Twin-Rivals, The Recruiting Officer, The Beaux' Stratagem)
MD 17 *Jean Racine: Five Plays* (Andromache, Britannicus, Berenice, Phaedra, Athaliah)
MD 18 *The Storm and Other Russian Plays* (The Storm, The Government Inspector, The Power of Darkness, Uncle Vanya, The Lower Depths)
MD 19 *Michel de Ghelderode: Seven Plays* Vol. 1 (The Ostend Interviews, Chronicles of Hell, Barabbas, The Women at the Tomb, Pantagleize, The Blind Men, Three Players and a Play, Lord Halewyn)
MD 20 *Lope de Vega: Five Plays* (Peribáñez, Fuenteovejuna, The Dog in the Manger, The Knight from Olmedo, Justice Without Revenge)
MD 21 *Calderón: Four Plays* (Secret Vengeance for Secret Insult, Devotion to the Cross, The Mayor of Zalamea, The Phantom Lady)
MD 22 *Jean Cocteau: Five Plays* (Orphée, Antigone, Intimate Relations, The Holy Terrors, The Eagle with Two Heads)
MD 23 *Ben Jonson* Vol. 2 (Every Man in His Humour, Sejanus, Bartholomew Fair)
MD 24 *Port-Royal and Other Plays* (Claudel: Tobias and Sara; Mauriac: Asmodée; Copeau: The Poor Little Man; Montherlant: Port-Royal)
MD 25 *Edwardian Plays* (Maugham: Loaves and Fishes; Hankin: The Return of the Prodigal; Shaw: Getting Married; Pinero: Mid-Channel; Granville-Barker: The Madras House)
MD 26 *Alfred de Musset: Seven Plays* (Marianne, Fantasio, Camille and Perdican, The Candlestick, A Diversion, A Door Must Be Kept Open or Shut, Journey to Gotha)
MD 27 *Georg Büchner: Complete Plays and Prose*
MD 28 *Paul Green: Five Plays* (Johnny Johnson, In Abraham's Bosom, Hymn to the Rising Sun, The House of Connelly, White Dresses)
MD 29 *François Billetdoux: Two Plays* (Tchin-Tchin, Chez Torpe)
MD 30 *Michel de Ghelderode: Seven Plays* Vol. 2 (Red Magic, Hop, Signor!, The Death of Doctor Faust, Christopher Columbus, A Night of Pity, Piet Bouteille, Miss Jairus)
MD 31 *Jean Giradoux* Vol. 2 (Siegfried, Amphitryon 38, Electra)
MD 32 *Kelly's Eye and Other Plays* by Henry Livings (Kelly's Eye, Big Soft Nellie, There's No Room for You Here for a Start)
MD 33 *Gabriel Marcel: Three Plays* (A Man of God, Ariadne, The Votive Candle)
MD 34 *New American Plays* ed. by Robert W. Corrigan (ten previously unpublished short plays)
MD 35 *Elmer Rice: Three Plays* (The Adding Machine, Street Scene, Dream Girl)
MD 36 *The Day the Whores Came Out to Play Tennis and Other Plays* by Arthur Kopit

MD 37 *Platonov* by Anton Chekhov
MD 38 *Ugo Betti: Three Plays* (The Inquiry, Goat Island, The Gambler)
MD 101 *Bussy D'Ambois* by George Chapman
MD 102 *The Broken Heart* by John Ford
MD 103 *The Duchess of Malfi* by John Webster
MD 104 *Doctor Faustus* by Christopher Marlowe
MD 105 *The Alchemist* by Ben Jonson
SD 1 *The Last Days of Lincoln* by Mark Van Doren
SD 2 *Oh Dad, Poor Dad, Mamma's Hung You in the Closet and I'm Feelin' So Sad* by Arthur Kopit
SD 3 *The Chinese Wall* by Max Frisch
SD 4 *Billy Budd* by Louis O. Coxe and Robert Chapman
SD 5 *The Devils* by John Whiting
SD 6 *The Firebugs* by Max Frisch
SD 7 *Andorra* by Max Frisch
SD 8 *Balm in Gilead and Other Plays* by Lanford Wilson (Balm in Gilead, Home Free!, Ludlow Fair)
SD 9 *Matty and the Moron and Madonna* by Herbert Lieberman
SD 10 *The Brig* by Kenneth H. Brown
SD 11 *The Cavern* by Jean Anouilh
SD 12 *Saved* by Edward Bond

CRITICISM

D 1 *Shakespeare and the Elizabethans* by Henri Fluchère
D 2 *On Dramatic Method* by Harley Granville-Barker
D 3 *George Bernard Shaw* by G. K. Chesterton
D 4 *The Paradox of Acting* by Denis Diderot and *Masks or Faces?* by William Archer
D 5 *The Scenic Art* by Henry James
D 6 *Preface to Hamlet* by Harley Granville-Barker
D 7 *Hazlitt on Theatre* ed. by William Archer and Robert Lowe
D 8 *The Fervent Years* by Harold Clurman
D 9 *The Quintessence of Ibsenism* by Bernard Shaw
D 10 *Papers on Playmaking* ed. by Brander Matthews
D 11 *Papers on Acting* ed. by Brander Matthews
D 12 *The Theatre* by Stark Young
D 13 *Immortal Shadows* by Stark Young
D 14 *Shakespeare: A Survey* by E. K. Chambers
D 15 *The English Dramatic Critics* ed. by James Agate
D 16 *Japanese Theatre* by Faubion Bowers
D 17 *Shaw's Dramatic Criticism* (1895-98) ed. by John F. Matthews
D 18 *Shaw on Theatre* ed. by E. J. West
D 19 *The Book of Job as a Greek Tragedy* by Horace Meyer Kallen
D 20 *Molière: The Man Seen Through the Plays* by Ramon Fernandez
D 21 *Greek Tragedy* by Gilbert Norwood
D 22 *Samuel Johnson on Shakespeare* ed. by W. K. Wimsatt, Jr.
D 23 *The Poet in the Theatre* by Ronald Peacock
D 24 *Chekhov the Dramatist* by David Magarshack
D 25 *Theory and Technique of Playwriting* by John Howard Lawson
D 26 *The Art of the Theatre* by Henri Ghéon
D 27 *Aristotle's Poetics* with an Introduction by Francis Fergusson
D 28 *The Origin of the Theater* by Benjamin Hunningher
D 29 *Playwrights on Playwriting* by Toby Cole
D 30 *The Sense of Shakespeare's Sonnets* by Edward Hubler
D 31 *The Development of Shakespeare's Imagery* by Wolfgang Clemen
D 32 *Stanislavsky on the Art of the Stage* trans. by David Magarshack
D 33 *Metatheatre: A New View of Dramatic Form* by Lionel Abel
D 34 *The Seven Ages of the Theatre* by Richard Southern
D 35 *The Death of Tragedy* by George Steiner
D 36 *Greek Comedy* by Gilbert Norwood
D 37 *Ibsen: Letters and Speeches* ed. by Evert Sprinchorn
D 38 *The Testament of Samuel Beckett* by J. Jacobsen and W. R. Mueller
D 39 *On Racine* by Roland Barthes
D 40 *American Playwrights on Drama* ed by Horst Frenz
D 41 *How Shakespeare Spent the Day* by Ivor Brown
D 42 *Brecht on Theatre* ed. by John Willett
D 102 *Theatre: Volume II* ed. by Barry Hyams